**The Alchemy Spoon
Issue 10**

The Alchemy Spoon
Issue 10

Editors
Roger Bloor
Vanessa Lampert
Mary Mulholland

Guest Editor
Tamsin Hopkins

A poetry magazine with a special interest in 'new phase' poets

Design and production
Clayhanger Press

Typeset in Times New Roman

Copyright
Copyright of all contents remains with the contributors
Copyright for design and images Clayhanger Press unless otherwise stated

Poetry Submissions
Our submission window is next open from 1 – 30 September 2023
The theme for the issue is 'Colours'

Please read the submissions guidelines on the final page
Submissions are through the website
www.alchemyspoon.org

Cover Images

Front Cover: *Off Shore*: acrylic, soft pastel & oil on paper by Sula Rubens
Back Cover: *On the seawall*: oil on canvas by Deb Catesby

ISSN 2635-0513
ISBN 978-1-7391770-6-5

We die to each other daily. What we know of other people is only our memory of the moments during which we knew them. And they have changed since then.

T.S. Eliot, *The Cocktail Party*

Contents

Editorial	Tamsin Hopkins	6
Herring girls	Elaine Ewart	8
News	Elaine Ewart	9
Fellowship	Hélène Demetriades	10
Travelling Companion	Ann Cuthbert	11
Toilet Rolls at Armageddon	Neil Douglas	12
Zippo	Chris Hardy	13
The Sex Lives of Dunnocks	Alexandra Corrin-Tachibana	14
The slight	Caroline Maldonado	15
On the union of cyanometer and sky	Sarah Doyle	16
Friend of the earth	Lesley Curwen	17
Watercourse with birds and logistics	Pascal Fallas	18
WomensLand	Jane Campbell	19
Bridesmaid	Claire Booker	20
In the National Trust tea garden	Anne Symons	21
Confessional	Sue Lewis	22
Outing	Julie Stevens	23
Let Me Introduce Myself	Matthew Caley	24
To Test Out Our Estrangement	Matthew Caley	25
Sundays on Parliament Hill	Zoë Wells	26
Come May	Sharon Ashton	27
Crossley Street	Martin Ferguson	28
flasher, 1991	Victoria Gatehouse	29
I Reply To A Text From My Best Friend Who Wants To Dance With Boys	Elizabeth Chadwick Pywell	30
Putney, 1983	Dave Wakely	31
CONSEQUENCES unexpected	Jeffery Sugarman	32
Lines following Amy Clampitt	Caspar Bryant	33
My houseparent is weeping on a rock	Matt Bryden	34
A Rug by Rachel Scott	Marc Chamberlain	35
I've got friends I only communicate with in reels	Jake Wild Hall	36
Neon	Steve Denehan	37
Brother-in-law	Philip Dunkerley	38
Nuptial bed	Wendy Klein	39
For the sake of the children	Finola Scott	40
Hawk	Jennifer A. McGowan	41
The hound	Cos Michael	42
I kept your vinyl & your long black scarf	Viv Fogel	43
Ice cream isn't the solution for everything, but it helps	Laura Stanley	44
Karan	Jen Feroze	45
The Back of You	Judith Wozniak	46
Portraits	Gillie Robic	47
A Personal View	Robin Houghton	48

The Interview	Mary Mulholland	52
Essay	Lesley Sharpe	61
The Reading	Elaine Ewart	67
Reviews		68
Reviews in Brief		92
Contributors		100
Pamphlet Competition		107
Submission Guidelines		108

Editorial

Out beyond ideas of wrongdoing
and rightdoing there is a field.
I'll meet you there
Rumi[1]

While I was delighted to be asked to guest edit this issue of *The Alchemy Spoon*, when I was told the theme had already been chosen and was 'Friends,' I had to think that over for a moment. I knew that I had only ever written one decent poem on that theme, and I realised I couldn't think of many. In fact, the poem by the American poet Eliza Griffiths that had inspired my poem was the only one that came to mind. I mentioned this. The ever-charming Mary Mulholland assured me we'd be inundated. She had got the idea for an issue themed on friendship after hearing Jonathan Edwards say that there were too few poems on this important subject. Nothing ventured, I thought, and we opened the floodgates.

Mary wasn't wrong. Poets wrote about more aspects of friendship than one poet (this one anyway) can expect to experience in a lifetime. There were poems circling special childhood friendships, friendships turned prickly, male friendship including one about the bond between brothers-in-law, female friendships (often involving tea, cake and/or booze), sexy friendships, dogs, betrayal, grief and loss. The poems were sometimes funny, often sad and wistful. Interestingly, not a single poem about friendship with work colleagues was received, although there was one about the army. And also our wonderful opening poem 'Herring Girls' by Elaine Ewart. So in fact there were two. I think I had expected that in real life, as in daft sitcoms, people make good friends at work. But if they do, they don't write about it much.

In the poems we received, the favoured form was couplets, followed by tercets. It was, in the main, not a theme which inspired intricate or traditional forms. As you will see, many poets wrote in a straightforward voice which spoke as though telling their friend something they wished they could say in person. Others, such as Matthew Caley, offered poems dealing with difficult emotional circumstances with a more delicate touch. Some came at their subject from an oblique angle. We received quite a few narrative poems and although not many of those made it to the final cut, the sense of lived experience, of a story behind the poem, was strong.

---

[1] https://poetrysociety.org/poetry-in-motion/out-beyond-ideas-of-wrongdoing-and-rightdoing

I loved reading these poems. It has been an absolute privilege to be trusted with your work. If this had been a competition, I would have asked for a special prize for 'most unusual and enjoyable poem' to be given to Neil Douglas for his poem 'Toilet Rolls at Armageddon'. But in truth this issue is stuffed with wonderful poems. I know you'll agree. I hope we'll see more good poems on this theme out and about, because, in the words of P.G. Wodehouse, 'There is no surer foundation for a beautiful friendship than a mutual taste in literature.'[2]

In this issue you will also find Mary Mulholland's interview with mother and daughter poets, Jean and Martha Sprackland. In her essay for this issue, Lesley Sharpe writes about 'recognition' in John Donne. The Personal View is Robin Houghton's experience of compiling her submissions spreadsheet. It's also a bumper issue for reviews of new titles from Julian Bishop, SK Grout, Wendy Kyle, Sue Wallace-Shaddad, and Diana Cant. Finally, our featured poet this time is Elaine Ewart and the link to her talk is on page 67.

Tamsin Hopkins

---

[2] P.G. Wodehouse from 'Strychnine in the Soup' in *Mulliner Nights*

Herring girls

Out of their element,
fish fly into barrels
at a rate of sixty per girl
per minute. Pulsing blood-red

        where brine works
        into wounds, women's hands
        gut and flick. Mired in slime,
        arms and aprons are

speckled with glinting scales.
Annie from Lewis has seen,
this season, two younger sisters
packed into boxes, dead of a fever.

        Go home, the others said, but she can't,
        with an empty purse. *Something in my eye*,
        says Annie. They chorus, *Don't touch it*.
        Tales of girls who went blind.

Let Mavis. Stout arms pin her by the shoulders.
Look up. Words breathed in her ear.
Keep them open! A gull flashes
across the sun. Warm muscle eclipses

        her eye. *Sorry, lass. Out now?*
        Annie ducks her head. Smell of oak wood
        smoke on the wind. Beneath
        closed lids, salt streams down.

Elaine Ewart

News

      'I'm pregnant,'
was almost an apology
congratulations fended off
    like a wet dog.

        I offer them anyway
          but they're strangers' words
    not what you say as your second self
breaks the tape
    you were running towards
        together.

    They say,
friends are the family you choose yourself.
    I'm unconsoled. I know
a baby pulls bloodlines taut
      mother to daughter.

    I give you a clumsy hug
and though you're barely twelve weeks gone
  we mind the ghost-space
of the child-to-be between us;
  hips apart
our shoulders lean towards each other
  my face hidden in your neck.

Elaine Ewart

Fellowship

Touched by a tiny white flower
I inherit the earth.

I've been tumbled under big skies,
a diaspore;

friends have been strewn
like drift nets on beaches.

I dig up a buried friend who says,
Eternity has no interest in chronology.

I dive into her words,
delight in our shared seabed.

Hélène Demetriades

Travelling Companion
(Ynes Mexia 1870 –1938)

In these photographs she frowns from makeshift jungle desk, inches across
a chasm-spanning log, dangles legs over Grand Canyon's rim.
My rebellious traveller. Nothing daunted her.

So slight, so unassuming, my Ynes. But tough as the boots she bushwacked in.
They told her women couldn't, especially not old ones, so she thought she better had –
for thirteen years, from Alaska to Tierra del Fuego, canoeing the Amazon,
camping in bogs, collecting her beloved specimens.

She didn't really need me, preferred solitude, but I tagged along,
braved earthquakes, sideways rain, unwashed hair,
took photographs while she took notes and measurements.

One hundred and fifty thousand plants, five hundred new species, fifty named for her.
'Something real and lasting,' she said.

My love for her.

Ann Cuthbert

Toilet Rolls at Armageddon

I have panic bought
and high shelves have emptied
into my cupboards, onto my stair,

the garage; overflowed to ceiling high —
a 3-ply flood lapping the cornice.
So, when the Electric goes I will,

alone in the dark, soak a Chosen One
in paraffin, set it aflame high atop
the lavatory brush to light the way

while, high on fumes, I build a bonfire
with Select Others to sizzle my last egg.
Then, only when all the food is gone,

and high as they are in natural fibre,
(though some have become companions,
friends), I shall consume them one by one.

Neil Douglas

Zippo

Isabel in a bikini.
Six of us round a jungle pool,
leaning on each other's shoulders
as boys do, mates, but no one
leans on her, tall,
smiling, a pineapple held
like a child or gift
before her belly
in both hands.

Monkeys and hornbills
hoot and croak
as we walk back
down the trail,
burning leeches
off our legs
with one last
Lucky Strike.

Chris Hardy

The Sex Lives of Dunnocks

You get distracted from a conversation
about how we'd like to declutter our lives,
wanting to test your bird song app, identifying
the song of a dunnock. Dunnocks, you say, peck
the bottoms of female birds to eject others' sperm.
And laughing, I say, *don't ever talk like that in front of
my friends*. And we talk again of feeling cluttered.
For me, part of it is a friend who wants me on tap,
says it's so long since we met, she's forgotten
what I look like. I talk of a *friendship edit*,
of freeing up headspace. Your clutter is what you call
life management: tax forms for flats in Madrid and a new
driving licence, now you've left your life in Spain,
to walk with me on Heathery Lane with our binoculars.

Alexandra Corrin-Tachibana

The slight

The closer the friend
the deeper the cut

even when delivered
with the lightest touch.

You can choose to parry
with your own hit

stab at her soft tissue
then try to forget

but her blade's poison
is in your bloodstream

raising your pressure
confusing the brain.

Hours, months, years
may pass until

the infection has truly
run its course.

Caroline Maldonado

On the union of cyanometer and sky

i. Cyanometer considers the sky

Roundel of possibilities, my unblinking eye
seeing only truths expressed in shades of blue:
sympathetic spectrum embracing a disc of sky
somewhere between zero and fifty-two.

ii. Sky considers the cyanometer

Empty iris seeking its fill, the toroidal twin
who completes the circle. How much blue
do we each contain? Measured from outside in,
equivalence: particles of me, particles of you.

Sarah Doyle

A cyanometer is an instrument for measuring the sky's blueness. It comprises an empty circle bearing 52 graduating shades of blue, so the sky may be observed through – and graded within – its window.

Friend of the earth

Let the seeds in the bread in my gut
burst through skin and soil to the sky.

Make me a haven of fecund rot
for the tendrils of weeds to climb.
    My bones, a scaffold of growth.

Let every cell of my meat spill
mineral sap into frazzled loam.

Make me a home for diligent germs
who pillage our essence for good.
    My heart, a substrate for love.

Lesley Curwen

Watercourse with birds and logistics

Wind roughed, cold toughened – and a kestrel
stuck to the sky. It could have been a case
of never to meet again, never to remember, yet
once more here we are after all, stalking stress
and the heady accents of old forms of discourse
like we'd just repaired broken sentences
from the last century. At our backs:
wing-blur, a skewering stare and the day
feels brighter than the year, brighter
than the lasting light of all these years.
Our stories remain mediocre but, to us, alive –
yet these days do we seem too alive
to our tight, overloaded bodies,
to our heavy thoughts that turn slow as barges,
then obscure as scraps of dream? The streaking cold
shine of this straightest stretch of water leads on
and our dusky kestrel springs ahead metres
at a time, to pin and repin its prey.
Now there are children who burn through
with their brash churn. And parents who grow old
and older still; who start to fail, to fall, to stick
in the wrong places. Maybe we grow too,
just a little way away from younger –
and does this also stick? Perhaps we are the prey
of time and our own glued-down ideas,
as on the horizon the cathedral carefully starts
to build itself into the sky. How we fill our minutes
seems to count now. No, no drink –
I moderate these days to a very specific amount
to keep the seeing straight, the outlook clear.
Mallards, geese in gaudy pairs, hypnotic threes.
As light starts to dim one small owl skirts
our inner flank and clock-thinking combs through
our words, straightening them out into a precise what,
a specific how. A buzzard cries – but the empty sky
holds only the tension of logistics and bearing loads.

Pascal Fallas

WomensLand

A circle of greening caravans,
trucks and hand-made shacks.

For fifty years, women have called this
high-ridge smallholding home.

I came to see what I looked like
with my wig off, my thorns pulled in.

Watched sisters cut their hair,
wield chainsaws and axes,

work together to coppice wood,
force shared fires to a red roar.

At first, I learned how to compost conflict,
honour my moon tides

until the day my final bloods were fed
to a favourite rose.

Now the sweat-lodge
beckons to our sky-clad skin and bones

and we crow-cackle our heart songs
long into the star-bright.

Jane Campbell

Bridesmaid

Claret and ivory: you've thought it through
       right down to the wedding favour.
             Three violets recline on the plump bed
     of your palm. So freshly picked
their saffron thumb-prints show.
       We clatter along ancient flagstones –
           you fluent in high heels, me clacking
     castanets, careful on the steps!
We join the groom hurrying to the millpond
       where you'll cast the violet thread
           across burgundy water
     in a ceremony of your own making.
I watch you hold hands, lean across our glassy triptych, deliver
       the frail bouquet to the pull of the sluice –
           it fractures the moon.

Claire Booker

In the National Trust tea garden

words tumble onto the table between us
   slide off the edge
      spill from the bench
         roll round our feet
            we are ankle-deep in words.

Some lie quiet in the dust
   homely and unpolished.
      Others, sharp-faceted
         scratch and make us bleed.

Some, like butterflies, escape too soon
   before we have a chance
      to appreciate their beauty.

I want to call them back
   feel the weight of them
      turn them over and say
         How so? and *What was that?*

I sweep them up
   fill all my pockets
      so in days to come
         I can take out a handful
            and hear your voice.

Anne Symons

Confessional

One hot and hollow day
let's take our skeletons to lunch –
I'll meet you by the Tube.

Blackening clouds, a sudden downpour:
intoxicating dark-earth scent
will rise from dust-dry pavements.

Sit with me. We'll share the wine.
Candles will bend forward to listen
though they've heard it all before.

Let's leave our shriven bones
inside that wine-dark cave.
Libate the final dregs.

Walk out to daylight and
a fresh breeze from the Thames.
Above us both, a clearing sky.

Sue Lewis

Outing

And if you're brave enough to ask, I will always come
though I may duck out early and leave you stranded.

And if we can't park nearby, in *THAT'S NOT FOR YOU!*
I will immediately transform into your volcanic nightmare.

And if I buy my cravings in a wonderful rush
know that you'll need that third arm to hold.

And when you breeze ahead, I will try to keep up
you may lose your neck, always looking behind.

And if you can't find me after ten minutes
I may not have told you, I'm over here, sitting down.

And when you're mastering another loud search
don't forget the toilets – enough said.

And if I stand on this dilemma and gossip too long
I may crash down and judge your panic.

And if I cancel our outing at the very last minute
know that I'm sure this will happen again.

Julie Stevens

Let Me Introduce Myself
after Stéphane Mallarmé – loosely

   and intrude upon your narrative   dear friend
the most feeble protagonist alive
afraid to step on a single grass-blade
in order to cross a clearing   a runway   and live
to think I've ransacked glaciers
in the past   maybe they were clouds?
it's true I cannot now think of a sin
you haven't resisted man-
   fully   even during our after-

   glow   [in retrospect]   and nor does it fill me with joy
to see sunset and lightning
   dazzle along this plane's

   engines and wing-span   the dropped jewellery
of a city below   speeding
   towards its own rusting and decline

so fast even those tiny cars might   carry me away

Matthew Caley

To Test Out Our Estrangement

   for the high of it   to seek summer air
you being so 'there' and yet not   the warm föhn of it
                sloughing and slaloming
the toxins hidden
presenting yourself as such
blowing through   cleaving to your cells   disappearing
as if touch could summarise
the bare stretches of night
   that insinuate between

   our thoughts   and we could get somewhere
the taut sand-lines of a beach
   looping and refreshing

   and erasing themselves   then see beyond that
for the sigh of it   an archipelago us: two flamingos
   on two separate sand-shelves

Matthew Caley

Sundays on Parliament Hill

She is the wind and I am a flag
our laughter whip-cracking
London carpeting the ground beneath our feet –
and each morning a familiar buzz beneath
my pillow, her message the welcome
alarm for the day

Zoë Wells

Come May

Up Willow Gardens, down Tom's Lane, we went
calling for friends, our lemonade gone flat,
our paste sandwiches squashed in paper bags.
Beguiled, all, by a green man and a horned
hunter, we crossed lawns edged with ragged daffs,
and tulips neat as scoops of pink kali
(that we dared each other to lick), then passed
into the ancient wood, watchful always
for Marion, Robin and Little John,
as we crunched down through leaves of years to find
the shady places, where bluebells massed dark
as skies in thunder, knowing how to tease
those slippery stems without breaking them.

Up Tom's Lane, down Willow Gardens, we came
home; arms aching with drooping sheaves of blue.

Sharon Ashton

Crossley Street

Bailey on rhythm acoustic,
Larby on drums, Locky on tambourine,
and Harby on piano–

a 1979 progressive education,
let loose to experiment, blissful
space in the primary school music room.

We were *The Dustbins,* ephemeral
as diluting rain of advancing years –
dark leviathan institutions
gathered over four horizons.

Martin Ferguson

flasher, 1991

it's an hour before dusk & our mouths are sweet
we chuck peel into the dappled shadows of laurels

my eyes are sore   I slip my lenses out & less
than a metre away a man is stripping off   I don't

realise he's there until my friend shifts   uneasy
he's watching   blurred against lush greenery

even without contacts I see   what he wants me to see
for the first three seconds it's almost funny   we

shuffle the length of the bench   oranges starting
to roll then   my friend yells *run like fuck* & she's up

her feet winged   mine splitting the soles to shoot
tarmac   seek earth   he's starkers & wreathed

in foliage & panic   is making a myth of this
walls close around cells   I'm half-way between girl

& tree when my friend hauls me up by the roots
he's gathering peel   we don't look back

the young policeman winks as he asks   did we
notice what he wore on his feet   *I wasn't looking at his*

feet my friend says & how we   piss ourselves
the same way I   joke about the second & the third

my friend & I lose touch   sometimes I think of her
when skirting that bend in the lane where laurels

hedge me in   one of the places I've learned to
quicken   how easy it is for   rustle to enter the breath

Victoria Gatehouse

I Reply To A Text From My Best Friend Who Wants To Dance With Boys

Edge the gym
Eye double doors

160 characters
repeat I'm not OK

Tell me later love
who you snogged

I'll say I don't care
Kiss my pillow

                                           ―――――
                                           ―――――
                                         getmeoutget
                                         meoutgetme
                                         outgetmeout
                                         getmeoutget
                                         meoutgetme
                                         outgetmeout
                                         getmeoutget
                                         meoutgetme
                                         outgetmeout
                                         getmeoutget
                                         meoutgetme
                                         outgetmeout
                                        ―――――
                                        ―――――

Elizabeth Chadwick Pywell

Putney, 1983

Tuesday mornings after signing on
we run the risk of friction burns
on your single bed's brushed nylon sheets
while Wonder Woman glares down disapproving
from your melamine wardrobe door.

Hands on hips like a mardy housewife,
more fish'n'chips than Stars and Stripes,
she still adds a top note of glamour
to our baser-reeking whiff. Clearasil
and cornershop cider: the classic
young male scent.

*Dad would say we should be bloody well
stoned for this*, you tell me, gleefully.
Too right, I nod, as green under the fingernails
as I am behind the ears, wondering how
one benefit cheque could ever cover
enough tobacco to comply.
And then you roll over, giggling,
those long brown fingers scratching
at the bright pink plaster that hide
that purple spot on your inner thigh
that never seems to heal.

Friday nights this summer, stood by your gate
while we mount bikes and leave for the common,
your Mum's turmeric-yellow anxious hands
fidget in her apron pockets. She is still ashamed
to smoke in front of us, her eyes
tennis-balling between our clothes and her watch.
Be home by midnight, she always says,
panic lingering under optimism.
*And will you ever put a jacket on?
One of these nights, you'll catch
your deaths.*

Dave Wakely

CONSEQUENCES *unexpected*

– after POSLEDICE [CONSEQUENCES],
a film by Darko Štante

He thinks they're his friends / these boys / who kiss speak a language / of no currency / but fists / He's fresh in detention / with a pet rat scratching / No one hears no one listens / the guards don't act / Who knew / queer boys / muscles made for silence / soft to touch / could unleash hell / that familiar hound / when trapped / even queer boys can be forced / to bodies they loath / lashed with irony / lashing out / like other men do / One bi-boy thug falls / to his knees / sucking cock / thick with blood Even the coarse / fill with love / it pours like air / into a pets' shoebox cage / to soothe / not gnaw / the hard night hard boys / mere boys / heads down / on kindergarten toys / blue plastic squats / turned to crazed fights cracked skulls / skunk weed / for forgetting / Two boys in / now kneeling in prayer / and ruptured balls / rent spleens / the cell-yard stacked / with fucked flesh

Jeffery Sugarman

Lines following Amy Clampitt

nomads enamored of cloverleafs, we
tangle in bedrooms as leaf meets twig,

an intimacy of the spine, insisting on our
constellation as just friends but it's

always morning when you're moving out, I
like to imagine dust when I'm sick of how

voices roll along the floor, of tongues held,
too warmly in the mouth, hot, filthy dust

building up in left-behind rooms. In a way,
our bodies are still only on loan, motion a

privilege of time, paid with the credit of jostling
cells, squishing organs, unbroken feet. What

do you think of a stem, which feeds and folds
flowers into each other, into stillness, not me –

Caspar Bryant

My houseparent is weeping on a rock

In his hand, the castanet of a mobile.
He could be calling his girlfriend in France
or fielding bad news from the family.
His crossed legs quite off the ground.

I pass along the gravel path and nod,
leave him to his traumas
as my eyes adjust to the field's dark.

Neither of us will mention this incident to the other.

Matt Bryden

A Rug by Rachel Scott
for Scott Midgley

'She flicked through the corners of a stack
then left me to it. Frank's sick in bed, she said,
and I need to take him up a cigarette.
Reckons she did this one around '67. When her eyes were keen.
See the detail.
Here, take these, give it a spray every now and then—
keeps the moths off.'
                        Your words taut as Rachel's weave
now under my feet at the desk, 'on long-term loan'
with you and Thomas away.
Memories as her coloured quadrilaterals—
     the drunken fumblings and the finer things,
          smoking with T out the backdoors,
               the three of us,
     driving through the rain in and out of the city—
'would've turned to dust by now without them.'

Marc Chamberlain

I've got friends I only communicate with in reels

how you been brother like alright still?
for sure life is just happening have you seen the one with the pan lid?
have you heard the one where they dub a man over a goat
yeah yeah I am the goat I am annie are you ok on ice
it's double tap it's hearts on our story hearts on our sleeve
it's 1am it's 6am it's do you ever sleep?
it's late shift morning shift memes no doubt
it's hugs on sight but it's spud it's touch it's I've got your back in a fight
I'm shit at Fifa but I'm that friend I'm drunk I'm drunk
do you need anything from the shop
yeah but I don't think you have the facilities for that big man
infinite ways to watch someone be hit in the head
infinite different items it can happen with
we've probably seen them all
we say lol a lot but it always means lots of love

Jake Wild Hall

Neon

We sat on the hillside
the city beneath us
the grass was not damp
but would be soon

you talked more than I did
which suited me fine
the usual stuff
nothings
and slightly smaller nothings

I knew something was coming
had felt a change in the air
before you paused and said
in not-quite-a-whisper
that your wife
no longer loved you

I gave it what I had
asked the right questions
offered evidence
tentative reassurance
while thinking
that it might be true

I told you to talk to your sister
to your mother
to your old friends

I told you to talk
to really talk
and really listen
to her

silence fell on us then
long seconds became long minutes

I looked at the faraway neon signs
in the shop windows
wanted to show you
how bright they were getting
in the seeping dark
but I figured
you would read something into it

Steve Denehan

Brother-in-law

On looking back, memory is mainly gaps, like water running between stepping stones,
and now that he's gone, the moment when we first met no longer really exists.
There are only the struts and spars of our relationship, on which hung patches and tatters
that, nevertheless, always had, when seen from a distance, a semblance of friendship.

But there really was a moment, an actual encounter, when our eyes met for the first time.
What did he make of me – unknown, different? What did I make of him? I don't remember.
Thereafter, chance and sporadic meetings, conversations when we respected the niceties,
each of us making context, getting along, avoiding friction, trying to work each other out.

Of course we'd always have known, had we stopped to think, that there would be an end,
that a day would come when half of everything would be torn utterly away and lost.
Who could say which way it would go and who would be left to draw conclusions?
That's a question whose answer, too late, I imagine he probably worked out for himself.

Philip Dunkerley

Nuptial Bed

It's silly o'clock here when you ring me
and even sillier o'clock where you are.
I am half-awake, the sky pinking up

outside my window, and straight off
you're on about how lonely you are
since your man died last year, how lucky

I am to have mine still. You're mad at me
for insisting that marriage, with all
its complicated paraphernalia of sex

and conversation, might not be
the best answer for loneliness.
Might it not be a better move, I ask,

to marry your bed – your own perfect bed,
chosen thoughtfully, the memory-foam mattress
that has mastered each and every zone

of your body: where your neck
gets stiff, where your lower back pain
starts? Think about its welcome:

reliable day or night, never cross
or rejecting. You could die
in that bed, be buried in it,

not even parted by death.
Is it legal, you ask?
And I know you are tempted.

Wendy Klein

For the sake of the children

we agree to be friends.
The reluctant rictus fixed
to my face fools no-one.

Not bound by a lawyer's contract,
our desolate tongues and
thorny thoughts range free.

Promises are easy to break – ask
Lot's wife, so much careless salt.
Ask Pandora, too much curiosity.

Romance slips down cracks.
Love & Hate dark tattooed
on my heart. Give and take dissolve.

Trying to remember the dancing,
laughing together, I watch the children
weave us friendship bracelets.

Finola Scott

Hawk

It's not every day you eyeball a sparrowhawk

and it looks back

yellow eye hostile
but not alien

like the girl in year 3
who said Jacqui stole you

& made the next six years
into a hell   fragmented
as any prey's breastbone

Jennifer A. McGowan

The hound

I am the dog that walks the woman
who woke up glazed and dressed slowly
I dance for her, but she isn't cheered
fumbling for keys and her lead
I bound from the door, willing her
to switch on her senses
sniff the ribboning trails of interest
swivel her ears to the morning choir
run circles in search of possibilities.
I guide my woman to the riverside
to play her eyes on the tumble and flow
but she looks at the water and weeps
I try to tug her towards the joy of squirrels
but she bends and slips her leash
I am the dog that rushes to and fro
frantically searching for presents,
while my woman slumps silent on a log
waiting for time to pass.

Cos Michael

I kept your vinyl & your long black scarf
(for Michael – in case it snowed ...)

You ask me to remind you of the snow   so that your sun-worn skin can
remember   cheeks pink with frosted breath   ice-crunch on hooded beck
leaves like lace beneath the glassy surface   on that starry last-night walk
.
Snow falls fast in unremembered places   smothers stories and cries
in unlit alleyways   drifts onto the forlorn and the fragile who slip
the shivering no-hopers

Deep snow covers blood   spit of phlegm   sodden condoms   fag ends
disrupts the quiet and the patient   sabotages those who plan who search
for excuses   settles on the resigned and the weary

* * *

You thought my snow would be a Disneyland of robins and reindeer   but
you settled for a land where it never snows   where bronzed bodies strut
beside chattering surf   or mottled and pre-cancerous   wait in torpid heat

You ask what I remember: a knitted patchwork quilt   on a creaking bed
(home-built)   our stifled laughter while others slept   a cold stone floor
powdery ashes in an un-swept hearth   the chill of dawn before you left

* * *

It's almost forty years now   we do not write   I heard you'd nearly died.
    When you visited last year   gaunt and spectral pale   your wild hair
            turned white   we sat at a distance   and you cried

    So I remember the betrayal of snow   and the choices we made:
            yours to follow the sun   mine a refusal to run

Viv Fogel

Ice cream isn't the solution for everything, but it helps

I stand at a freezer in Tesco Express – gooey caramel or chocolate fudge brownie? which one tastes best like I love you, like I'm sorry, like I will never be able to thank you enough times, thank you, thank you, for always opening your door to me when I was shaking and crying, for calling me a taxi and saying my friend is unwell, she's taken some pills, yes, I'll stay with her, for sitting with me in A&E, for lying on the cold hospital floor so I wasn't alone and staying until 2AM, for sitting with me in A&E again one week later, for sharing your earphones, one bud each, our heads pressed together, watching a candyfloss rom-com from the noughties on the last dregs of your phone battery when I needed a distraction from wanting to smash my head on a sink, for all those days when I was too tired to even talk, when I didn't have the strength to hug you back as tight as you hugged me, when I would never want to be my friend and, for moments like now, when you ask me how I'm doing after I knock on your door and give you two tubs of Ben & Jerry's

Laura Stanley

Karan

I know how tired you are but look,
see how the winter trees wait for you,
barefaced with longing. How the puddles
adorn themselves with haloes of crystal,
glittering shyly along muddied paths.

Below ground there are snowdrops –
envoys of the spring that tantalises
just out of reach, tangled in branches like a kite
made of light and warmth. Have faith in its coming
as the birds do. See how they are returning to these same trees,
how the copse applauds your fortitude with sudden, beating wings.

Most of all, see how a small hand
is clutched by a smaller one at the edge of the pond,
how pillars of frosted breath intermingle
(breath you forged from your own, deep fire).
How, when their blond heads are bent together,
just for a second, they could be saplings
intertwined.

Jen Feroze

The Back of You

I must have taken it with my Brownie camera.
A black and white snap, the back of you
in a baggy dress, a tangle of unruly curls.
I'm following you through the prickly grass
path from your farm to the old quarry,
out of bounds, across a disused railway line
to watch your brother play 'dare' with the boys.
We often smuggled cake from the pantry,
wrapped in hankies, tucked in our pockets.
My mother, staying with your aunt
in the big house, had no idea where
we were. You always looked out for me,
shouted at the boys who called me Queenie,
mimicking my Essex twang.
Do you remember those plays we put on?
Dressed up in your aunt's negligees,
floaty scarves and beads. I think the line
about taking a lover put a stop to it.
I overheard my mother whisper, *those two!*
Too old for Noddy, too young for Lolita.
Years later I heard you'd run away,
left your home and job. Nobody would say
what became of you. I saw you once,
at your aunt's funeral, elegant in black.
I tried to catch your eye but your face
was hidden under a broad brimmed hat.

Judith Wozniak

Portraits
(after Howard Hodgkin)

Some of my friends
fit the room, touch it with orange impasto.

Some exist in their likeness, leave me
outside, searching the streets.

Some are woven, textured,
not imposing but belonging.

Some lurk on the edge, implicit,
framed but not pulling focus.

Some jar their own instability
onto foldaway scenes, command loudly.

Some of my friends
are vector and pattern, the colour of dance.

Gillie Robic

A Personal View

Robin Houghton reflects on the development of her popular monthly spreadsheet of poetry submission opportunities and the podcast *Planet Poetry*.

Like many poets I can trace my earliest attempts at writing back to my schooldays. But it was decades later, when my career was winding down, that I started reading contemporary poetry, and got the urge to try writing it seriously. I had my first poem published in 2010 and took it as a sign that I should carry on.

That was when I began submitting more systematically to poetry magazines. I love a spreadsheet and was keen to track everything: poems submitted/accepted/declined, response times and so forth. Then a trend emerged: magazines started to close their 'always open' policies in favour of reading windows, and any submissions outside of those windows would not be considered, a trend which has now become the norm. I had to start keeping track of submissions windows, so I built a more detailed spreadsheet. And if I was doing it for myself, why not share it?

I had been email-marketing since the early 2000s and blogging and tweeting since 2006. So building and promoting an email list was second nature. There was a saying among early adopters of the internet: *information wants to be free.* I was one of those early adopters. It was a real community: optimistic, generous, non-commercial. I'd fallen in love with all this when I was living and working in the US in the 1990s, so much so that I left my marketing career to come back to the UK and work in 'online marketing' (a term hardly known then). The web has been my livelihood, for sure, but in my heart I still believe in sharing at least some stuff for free.

I first mailed out the submissions windows spreadsheet in 2017, and it has grown to include over 200 journals: mostly UK and Ireland, but I'm including international online magazines too. I include a live link to the web address of each journal's submissions page, its publishing schedule, what they are looking for, submissions method and so forth. Every quarter I trawl the web and update the spreadsheet to say which magazines are open now, how long for, current themes, and whether anything has changed. I'm always on the lookout for new journals to replace those that disappear: each quarter I lose about 5% of titles. It's never going to be an exhaustive list, and I tell people that. I do a certain amount of curating. A couple of journals have never been on the list. I have my reasons, and no, it's not because they have rejected my poems!

I'm mostly dependent on editors keeping their web presence up to date. If the website isn't clear, I go to Twitter or Instagram. Quite often the socials get updated before the website. Having said that, I never consult Facebook. If a magazine only exists on Facebook then that's their choice to cut themselves off from the rest of the online world! If a website and its social feeds have been inactive for six months or more, I sometimes contact editors to find out what's going on. However, this is a huge time suck, and a query rarely results in a reply, so I generally only do that if it's a long-established journal and/or I know the editor. Small magazines come and go with great frequency. This was particularly the case during the pandemic years. There are one or two 'friendly' editors who keep me updated without my having to ask, but mine is undoubtedly a service for poets, not the magazines themselves. Some editors probably wish I would stop encouraging submissions!

Nevertheless, I am a champion of small magazines. Editing a poetry magazine is often a thankless task, and if nobody were prepared to do it, where would we get our poems published? Yet I can lose patience sometimes. Any editor inviting submissions *must* have in place a robust system for dealing with them. *The Alchemy Spoon* clearly does. Many do not. Enough said!

Back in 2000 someone said to me *people would pay money to know what you know*, and that thought has stayed with me since. So in 2018 I combined my experience of writing 'how to blog' manuals with what I had learned from eight years of submitting poems and published a booklet, *A Guide to Getting Published in UK Poetry Magazines*. In 2020 I produced a second updated edition, which sold out in a few months. I am sure a big part of the booklet's appeal was the fact that I had asked a dozen or so editors to contribute their thoughts and nuggets of advice. I also showcased many magazines with pictures of their covers, details of editors and the names of poets they had published. Maybe there will be another edition, who knows!

Meanwhile, updating and distributing the spreadsheet has become quite a big job now, especially as I also email everyone at the end of each month with a reminder of windows about to close. It is an entirely free service, and I want to keep it that way. However, around six months ago I was on the verge of giving it up: my list was too big for the free version of Mailchimp, and maintaining the list was costing time *and* money. That was when I decided to set up a donations page at buymeacoffee.com – and moved the list to a better value email provider. I should have done it sooner. Not only does the Buy me a Coffee page help by paying my monthly costs, it also means I get more one-to-one contact with people on my list, which I enjoy.

In 2020, given the year that it was, I needed more projects. So I did two things. Firstly I enrolled on an MA in Poetry and Poetics at the University of York. I knew I didn't want to do a creative writing MA. I wanted to learn more about that huge iceberg of poetry that sits beneath my flimsy efforts. I read Virgil and Ovid, I fell in love with Dante and Chaucer, I got to understand T.S. Eliot and Tennyson a bit better. I even wrote a term paper entitled 'From *Dictee* to *Nox*: artifice, artefact and hybrid form'. No kidding.

The second thing I started that year was podcasting. During that first lockdown I was talking to poet pal, Peter Kenny (who I had collaborated with in the past on Telltale Press), and he mentioned the idea of a podcast. Amazing! I'd been thinking the very same thing. And it was a perfect pandemic activity – all done remotely from home. Before we knew it we were searching 'how to start a podcast', checking out the equipment needed and discussing what we were going to call it.

I should probably go back a step here and explain about Telltale Press. In 2013 I was on a residential course and Carol Ann Duffy was one of the tutors. Several of us were frustrated at the lack of opportunities to get a first pamphlet published, and Carol Ann suggested we start our own press, to publish our own short pamphlets and use them as 'calling cards' to help get our work known.

I discussed the idea with Peter, whom I had met at the Brighton Stanza, and I knew that he, like me, felt ready for a pamphlet. So Telltale Press was born. We asked Catherine Smith to be our Editorial Advisor, and Carol Ann Duffy agreed to be our Patron. We called it a 'poets publishing collective', we held readings and we published and launched five pamphlets in all. Although in theory all members contributed to the running of the press, in reality it proved a bit impractical. We had exciting plans, including a roadshow which was going to combine readings with workshops on how to set up a publishing collective. But I think the monumental task of putting together a modest bid for ACE funding, only to have it refused, wore me down. We finished with an anthology of work on the theme of 'truths' and the contributors were all poets who had read at our events.

Although we closed the collective, I'm very proud of what we'd achieved. Poets who began their publishing career with Telltale went on to have books with publishers such as Smith|Doorstop, Nine Arches, Cinnamon and Live Canon. Telltale is dormant rather than dead – it might well rise again from the ashes.

Peter and I launched *Planet Poetry* in October 2020 and we are about to start our fourth season in October 2023. The format is simple – one of us interviews a poet (or poets) about their work, then Peter and I chat about the interview, share what we have been reading, and discuss the poetry world. We like to banter, and we talk about our own experiences. It's very informal – we take poetry seriously but not ourselves. So far, we've interviewed fifty guests from ten different countries, so it feels like a big planet!

The practicalities of putting together a podcast on a shoestring can be frustrating: dodgy internet connections or other tech issues, pinning poets down to dates and times they are free, software hitches. Each episode involves hours of editing. We have tried to keep to a two to three week publishing schedule, but with family and work commitments it hasn't always been possible. But we don't think our listeners mind. We've had some good coverage in *Poetry News*, and the number of regular listeners and downloads is steadily increasing, particularly since the beginning of 2023. We recently launched a Buy me a Coffee donations page, and we look forward to the day when we're no longer funding *Planet Poetry* out of our own pockets.

As regards the MA at York, although I completed the first year and absolutely loved it, I was fed up with all the Zooming. In 2021–22 I took a year's sabbatical, but decided not to continue with the second year. I was just too busy with other things, and it took up a vast amount of time and intellectual energy.

At the moment I'm submitting poems now and then, but not writing a lot of new poetry, mainly because my project for 2023 is to write a novel. In fact, the first draft is done and I'm close to sending it out. Will it ever be published? Wish me luck!

Robin Houghton

robinhoughtonpoetry.co.uk
planetpoetrypodcast.com

The Interview

Mary Mulholland talks to mother and daughter poets, **Jean** and **Martha Sprackland** about their individual and shared experiences.

Jean started writing poetry seriously at thirty, became professor of Creative Writing at Manchester Metropolitan and has been shortlisted for the Forward, T.S. Eliot, Whitbread and Pen Ackerley Prizes and won the Costa Prize. She has published five collections and has worked as an editor, publisher and translator. Martha has written two pamphlets and a collection and been shortlisted for the Forward, John Pollard International and Costa awards.

MM: Jean, did you come from a literary family, had there been writers in the family, were you encouraged?

Jean: Oh no, definitely no writers in the family. But both my parents were great readers. My dad came from a family of tenant farmers, but he broke away from that life, took himself to college and became a librarian. That was a real gift for my brothers and me. It meant that we always had books, though we didn't actually own many – it was a culture which taught me that literature was a communal thing.

My mum loved poetry. I remember I wrote a poem for school homework – it was about winter, and included a line about 'silver snowflakes'. She said 'But they're not really silver, are they? Don't just write what *sounds* nice – you have to really look.' It was a simple and invaluable piece of writing advice which I've carried with me ever since.

I discovered poetry in a rather random and unsupervised way through anthologies I happened to find lying about. In a dusty heap on a classroom windowsill there was a series called *Voices*, edited by Geoffrey Summerfield, which featured poems by children alongside famous names past and present. They had surreal illustrations and weird page numbering, and they evoked in me a powerful feeling of freedom that from then on I associated with poetry.

I always wrote poems, but it wasn't until I was thirty that I woke up and paid attention to them. I ended up on an Arvon course at Lumb Bank, which changed everything: poetry and writing moved to the very centre of my life.

MM: Martha, I read you had your first poetry success at about seven, and went on your first Arvon week at eleven. How impactful was this?

Martha: That early poetry success was perhaps the poetry category at the Ainsdale Village Show, run by the local horticultural society. Social event of the year! I didn't do too badly in the miniature flower arrangement category, either (my brother used to clean up in the baking category). It encouraged creativity – not just in writing, but in making physical things – and taking creativity seriously. I have a poem in *Citadel* about going out to the dunes at five a.m. with my dad to find a scarlet pimpernel, which I'd read about in books and decided had to be in my miniature flower arrangement entry. Both my parents understood the importance of those impulses.

The Arvon week when I was eleven was incredibly special. It was the prize for being a winner in the Foyle Young Poet of the Year Award (which then was called the Simon Elvin Prize). Nowadays I don't think the youngest of the cohort go on the Arvon week – so I was very lucky, and lucky that Jean and my dad understood the worth of it. It was taught by Peter and Ann Sansom. I remember it being very focused and heady and new. It felt like a real initiation. I sat under the table in the library and wrote poems; the group introduced me to poems by Bishop and Hughes and Plath and more, and also taught me how to cook a fried breakfast.

MM: How difficult is it to be daughter/mother working in the same metier? How do you overcome comparisons with one another?

Jean: I suppose some people do make comparisons, but I steer away from that kind of conversation more generally. I need a lot of empty space, I need to be able to hear myself think, I can't write if my head is buzzing with who said what about my work or someone else's. But in any case I'm blown away by Martha's work, in a way that far exceeds the usual maternal pride – she achieves things I know I never could and never will.

Martha: I don't think people ever really do compare us, do they? I don't think our writing is very similar, though we have shared concerns. The place where we do overlap, in terms of subject matter, is the landscape of the northwest coast of England. We've both written about that, from different points of view. We're both interested in it as a place, its strangeness, but I'm sure that my experience of it – living there as a child then a teenager – was different to Jean's experience of it, coming to the place as an adult with a new baby. I feel connected to the scrubland, the arcades, the pine woods, the bits behind the rec, the dens and hiding places in the dunes – all the places children roam and teenagers claim. Jean writes so powerfully about the beach, in the poetry and also in *Strands* – though it's not so clean a division as all that!

MM: Jean, did you try to shield your daughter from the poetry world you were in, or actively encourage her?

Jean: I don't think I could have shielded either of my kids from the poetry world. When I was involved in readings and workshops I often took them along, and occasionally poets would stay at our house. Martha probably remembers Matthew Sweeney re-naming our pet rabbit and taking me to task about my method of cooking porridge…

Martha: I don't remember anything about porridge!

Jean: I like to think I encouraged her. I couldn't have foreseen that she would make a life in writing, but looking back it's not surprising, because she was exceptionally interested in it from an early age, and by the time she was a teenager that interest had evolved into something more like a vocation.

MM: Martha, growing up did you understand what your mother's work was? Did you read it, like it, or feel excluded?

Martha: I thought of Jean's job as 'teacher', when I was young, before realising she was a writer. Her first book must've come out when I was about nine or ten, and I was very impressed – it brought home to me the exciting fact that books (which I loved) were written by *people* – and that I could be someone who wrote a book. There was one of her poems in a frame on the wall in our hallway – a postcard produced for some event or other – called 'Deadnettle', and I used to read that through entire, quickly, almost every time I passed it. I liked it because I knew what deadnettle was, and because it was intriguing to me to imagine Jean as a child, and because it's a good poem – it still lives in my head.

MM: Does competitiveness ever feature? What are your unfulfilled poetry ambitions?

Jean: I don't know how it feels for Martha, but I don't feel any competitiveness. To be outdone by your child is surely a joy for any parent – it is for me, anyway. I love celebrating her successes and seeing her blaze her own trail. Poetry can be a small world, but it's also a capacious one and there are different ways of being in it. Perhaps we cultivate a little separation. For example we very rarely do things jointly – this interview is an exception!

My unfulfilled poetry ambition is the same as it's always been: to write the next poem.

Martha: It's never come up! We've never had a book out in the same year, luckily. And it helps that we've carved out slightly different places in the poetry world – I've always worked in editorial, in publishing, whereas Jean is a lecturer at a university. We've both taught on Arvon courses, though not together. We don't tread on each other's toes. When she was invited recently to be the chair of judges for the T.S. Eliot Prize she did have to text me before agreeing to do it and say 'Er – you're not planning to publish a book this year, are you?' I wouldn't want to compete. I think Jean's writing is incredible – I'd be reading her as a fan if I wasn't reading her as a proud daughter.

Jean: I think Martha has always had a stronger sense of direction than I did. I stumbled into university teaching somewhat by accident, having spent the previous fifteen years working for the Poetry Archive, the Poetry Society and other literature organisations. I didn't have a plan, I just liked having a working life that revolved around poetry and poets. The two of us each have our areas of expertise.

Martha: Currently my unfulfilled poetry ambition is just to write enough good poems for another book – it's been a thin couple of years.

MM: What do you understand by the 'poetic gift'?

Martha: I always get a little impatient when people talk about 'the muse', or poetic inspiration, but in softer moods I suspect we're all talking about different things when we use those words. I'm fine with the concept of 'having an idea for a poem', of course, and certainly I agree that it can come at any time, under any circumstances, and can sometimes feel as if it arrives *as if from nowhere*. But an idea only ever comes from the writer, not from some external force. And the writing itself, the committing of the idea to the page – that's a kind of wonderful work.

As far as the poetic gift goes, I think the best poets are simply good editors of their own work. Some do their editing as they write the poem, meaning that their first drafts come out like tenth drafts. Some do their editing through successive versions. But that diligence in going back to the poem, returning to the words and the lines and the rhythm and the sound and the levels and layers and patterns – all of that is part of the poetic gift. Some people catch the knack of it easier, but those skills can be taught. Whenever I've taught a poetry class or course or workshop that's what the students always want to focus on – editing, redrafting, reworking.

MM: How conscious is your choice of 'I'll write this as poetry/prose'?

Jean: I started writing prose non-fiction as a way of making space to follow an investigative trail which I couldn't fit into a poem. It grew out of an obsession with a particular stretch of the northwest coast, between Southport and Formby, and objects I found there on my long walks on the beach. They had already found their way into my poetry, but I wanted to look at them through a different lens. Poems are hungry things that devour and transform what we feed into them, sometimes quite violently – but that's what makes them special, their capacity to transcend subject matter. Prose offers a degree of detachment that allows me to consider it in a different way.

Martha: It takes a conscious effort to write prose that isn't too 'poetic'. And it's difficult. Because you're used to noticing all sorts of things, that if you put them all in a novel would be ten thousand pages long. Fiction takes restraint. Poetry does, too, of course – you can't just put everything in. It takes practice to learn the different skills of fiction. They're not so different really – strictly speaking there's nothing you can do in one that you can't do in the other. You can be as abstract or narrative as you like, use whatever form you like, move from one thing to another however you want to. One kind of fiction I often enjoy, and wish I could write, is not like poetry at all; it's vast, realist, immersive – I like big novels in which the only things that happen are between people, their dialogue, their misunderstandings, their growth and change, the long view of a life or family or cohort. And that's less easy to accomplish in a poem.

MM: Many poets say their families and 'other world' friends are disinterested in their poetry, which may be isolating yet liberating. Since your experience is the opposite, do you read or give feedback on each other's work in progress?

Martha: Sometimes we do, especially when we've been asked to write a poem for a commission. Because the 'idea' or theme or requirement comes from somewhere else it can be harder to tell whether the poem is good.

Jean: For a long time I was in that 'isolating yet liberating position' and all poets have to go out and find trusted early readers for their work, whether through workshops, informal groups or individual friendships with other writers. In the early days, much of that happened for me with the incredible network of poets I got to know in Liverpool, and there are others I've formed this kind of mutual link with since.

Martha and I do sometimes read each other's drafts – perhaps when we want feedback quickly or on something specific. It's great for me, because her experience as an editor and publisher makes her a really acute reader – if there's a dodgy metaphor or a clunky bit of phrasing, she'll spot it.

MM: What gets you writing? And do you write better alone or within groups? Do you belong to writing circles?

Martha: I'm in a workshop group with six poet-friends – we try and meet every couple of months at one of our houses and each bring one poem. I used to go to Roddy Lumsden's Wednesday group, which is where I met some of those poets, actually. I think advice from people whose opinion you trust, whose taste you respect, and whose own poems you like, is essential.

Things that get me writing – oh, quite basic things. Having a clear break from work – being a poetry editor makes writing poetry more difficult. Weirdly, I've noticed I write interesting things when I'm ill, or particularly hungry or tired – some kind of physiological pressure on the mental processes. I always write better when I'm away from home. And I have ideas for poems when I read other people's poems, so I do that as much as I can – like going to the well.

MM: What about translations?

Martha: Translation, writing poetry and editing books all feel like aspects of the same basic impulse, which is that I love fiddling with word choices until a piece of text *feels* right. I've recently been translating some of the poems of San Juan de la Cruz, or Saint John of the Cross, a sixteenth-century mystic poet from Ávila, and the work is absorbing in part because of the way rhyme works differently in Spanish to the way it does in English – verb conjugations in Spanish, as well as gendered endings, make a difference – and bringing something like that into English is like a puzzle, something you work on and think about and pick at and obsess over until there's a *click* and the stanza suddenly works. Like writing poems in the first place.

MM: What are your views on accessibility vs making the reader work – how do you find the dividing line?

Jean: I think clarity and mystery are both vital, and the tension between them is the most exciting work of the poet. The poems I love best are as clear as water, yet do not give up on the mysterious. When I'm writing I try to identify and locate the mystery, which frees me to make everything else in the poem as clear as possible.

Martha: Unless you're going to write down an anecdote or observation in completely plain, informative English, unembellished, without metaphor, allusion, description, pattern or play, then there'll be some role for the reader. When I read poetry, I like to have to think about it a bit. One of the things poets who are just starting out struggle with is trusting the reader to do that work – they're anxious to be understood. So they might title a poem 'My Grandmother's Purse' or something and then end the poem with the lines 'and that is why I will always treasure / my grandmother's purse – *because it belonged to her*'. And that's just giving away the farm. It's not interesting to read. Luckily it's a really easy thing to fix.

MM: Given that so much poetic material can be drawn from family/childhood is this something that limits/inhibits you? Memory also plays tricks: how different are your shared biographical experiences?

Jean: Such an interesting question. Memory is a rich seam for both of us. But memory is notoriously partial and fallible, and I wouldn't expect the two of us to agree on a single version of events, any more than my mother and I would have.

Autobiography gets fused with fiction, in writing and in life – that's particularly true of childhood, which has an especially dreamlike quality in the memory.

When I read something of Martha's that draws on childhood, I notice the autobiographical elements and recall them myself, while at the same time reading it as a piece of literature in which lived experience has been alchemised into something more than itself. As a writer myself I know this process from the inside, so I never think 'Hang on, Martha, that's not what happened!'.

Martha: Perhaps I would be wary of relating in poetry a conversation between the two of us that happened when I was a child, just in case I'd misremembered it! Though interestingly, that's part of what that poem of Jean's, 'Deadnettle', is about – a conversation between mother and daughter.

MM: What ways do you recommend writing about difficult material and narrative?

Martha: I have a little postcard in my office with a quote by Edna O'Brien: *'The thing which a writer should never do is withdraw.'*

MM: Who are your go-to poets?

Martha: It's always hard choosing 'favourite' or go-to poets – inevitably if you're reading constantly and widely that's going to be in flux. I'll just mention new things: I've admired Maggie Millner's *Couplets* and Emily Hasler's *Local Interest*, Toby Martinez de las Rivas's new book *Floodmeadow*, as well as Declan Ryan's debut *Crisis Actor* which is out this summer. And of course there are poets I publish – Sarah Fletcher's debut *PLUS ULTRA* and Kandace Siobhan Walker's forthcoming *Cowboy* are both wonderful. I've been looking forward to *Isdal* by Susannah Dickey and *The Recycling* by Joey Connolly – both out this year. In Spanish, I really admire Rodrigo García Marina, whose *Desear la casa* came out a couple of years ago.

Jean: I like fiery women poets who write with candour, guts and humour: Sharon Olds, Vicki Feaver and Denise Riley, to name but a few. I still go back to poets I fell in love with in my schooldays: Sylvia Plath, Emily Dickinson, T.S. Eliot, Louis MacNeice. At the same time there's been a real explosion of energy and plurality in the past ten years, and I try to find a balance – too much emphasis on the 'go-to' can stop us reading what's being published now and making new discoveries.

MM: Do you have any advice/ suggestions for our readers, many of whom have come to poetry following other careers?

Martha: Make sure you *use* what you bring from that previous career – that material is gold!

Mary Mulholland

Publications by Jean Sprackland

Spike
Tattoos for Mother's Day (1997)

Jonathan Cape
*Hard Water (*2003*); Tilt* (2007); *Sleeping Keys* (2013); *Green Noise* (2018)

Cape
Strands (2012); *These Silent Mansions* (2020)
https://www.jeansprackland.com

Publications by Martha Sprackland

Pavilion Press
Citadel (2020)

Rough Trade
Milk Tooth (2020)

Rack Press
Glass as Broken Glass (2016)
https://www.marthasprackland.co.uk

Essay

'Some lovely glorious nothing': **Lesley Sharpe** considers the quality of recognition in poems by John Donne and Edwin Muir.

If recognition and immanence touch the essence of friendship, then it seems to me that the first lines of John Donne's poem 'Air and Angels'[1] capture this sense of closeness. The poet makes an emphatic, and moving, opening gambit: 'Twice or thrice had I lov'd thee/ Before I knew thy face or name', launching the poem into a multiple frame of reference that plays to both his innate Catholic sensibility – the religious iconography of his youth – and a Platonic idealism in which the body of the beloved can be apprehended in its ideal form, the beautiful long assonance of 'shapeless flame' full of the brightness of such an encounter. In addition, the extended simile which follows weaves in a Petrarchan preoccupation with the divine in its secular and romantic aspect, an ideal of courtly love that can elevate the beloved into a rarified, otherworldly creature, while pursuing more earthly designs.

Those small repeated words, 'so in' – 'So in a voice, so in a shapeless flame' – lift us into the heart of the poem, dominating the first stanza and accumulating a presence which underpins the connection being described. They create an easy movement to a world where 'Angels affect us oft and worshipped be'. The beguiling simplicity of the language and its precision, its sense of brightness and rhythm, plays with the way language can be used to embody that which can be imagined:

> Still when, to where thou wert, I came,
> Some lovely glorious nothing I did see.

Yet this is a poem that keeps its feet firmly on the ground:

> But since my soul, whose child love is,
> Takes limbs of flesh, and else could nothing do,
> More subtle than the parent is
> Love must not be, but take a body too;

The argument of the poem takes another turn, moves out of the realm of romance by introducing the dynamic of parent and child to

---

[1] Air and Angels by John Donne | Poetry Foundation   John Donne, Poems (1633)

explore ideas of causality, and also the possibility for what the thirteenth century theologian Thomas Aquinas called 'the mixed life', of both contemplation and action, captured in Donne's witty use of 'do'. Thus, an apparently dialectical approach can ensue, by which to rationally approach the beloved:

> And therefore what thou wert, and who,
>   I bid Love ask, and now
> That it assume thy body, I allow,
> And fix itself in thy lip, eye, and brow.

Here we find more of Donne's layered imagery, where the 'lip, eye and brow' seem at once to be playing to conventional Petrarchan imagery, where the beloved is so indistinct as to be generic, a sentiment at odds with the insistent particularity captured in the opening line of the poem. The ambiguous multiplicity of 'twice or thrice', however, to describe angelic visitation, is almost casual in its reckoning – who wouldn't remember exactly how many times? There is also the lingering sensuality of those 'limbs of flesh'. Simultaneously Donne is engaging with the way an angelic being can take form and manifest itself in and to the human realm, according to the medieval world whose philosophy he inherited. Air, being the purest of the elements, but lower than the angelic beings in the great chain of being which defined the medieval universe, is now the medium for this transformation from 'glorious nothing' to physical reality.

This is angelic being as fierce intelligence positioned above man, but the verb 'fix' here is also at odds with the mutable nature of both 'air', and, as will later be explored in the poem, the alchemy of human affection in its male and female aspects. To add another layer of complexity, angels were understood mostly to be male – think Gabriel, the messenger, or archangels Michael and Raphael. Or they were possessed of a kind of gender neutrality, above and beyond the distinctions of sex. So why did Donne choose this iconography to explore a poem about human, sexual love, weaving into it so many other resonances?

The poem was first published in 1633 in *Poems*, though written earlier, and engages with what might have seemed an easy convention that men occupy a higher spiritual position than women. Perhaps by using the distinction between 'angels' and 'air', one (superior) taking form through the other (inferior) – nearly, but not quite, identical – Donne can introduce, in the midst of perfect recognition, an almost indiscernible tension, an image which can be used later to also capture the complexity of desire. Developing the analogy, he considers the best medium for his own feelings of love to be manifested. What about his lover's body? – 'perhaps to ballast love I thought,/ And so more steadily to have gone'. As Katherine Rundell writes in *Super-Infinite: The Transformations of John Donne*, 'he kicked aside the Petrarchan traditions of idealised, sanitised desire: he joyfully brought the body to collide with the soul'.[2] But its complex relation to the body is his constant preoccupation. For him love is a mixture of elemental things, 'as all else being elemented too' ('Love's Alchemy'). For all its mood of transcendence, love must fulfil its physicality, 'else a great prince in prison lies' ('The Exstasie').

In 'Air and Angels', Donne explores how these two apparent opposites, body and soul, might find their middle ground, 'For, nor in nothing, nor in things/ Extreme, and scatt'ring bright, can love inhere'. But, extending ideas of hierarchy, the beloved's body, 'love's pinnace' (a small ship going out from the main ship) would be overloaded by the strength of his feeling, with 'wares which would sink admiration', not the compatible medium for his pure love at all. The wry pun in pinnace (penis) shouldn't go unnoticed, however, nor the seventeenth century association of these small boats with the precarious, and exciting, exploration of new worlds.

Donne's argument leads him away from an obvious hierarchy into the new, and somewhat abstract, world of science, to conclude that he must encircle her: 'So thy love may be my love's sphere', exploring the ways in which two aspects might find themselves in one relation. The woman is also perhaps more specific in her immanent presence than in her realised form, hinting at a process of becoming that is never complete. As modern readers we might object to the apparent misogyny of Donne's conclusion – men are like angels, women like air – or take this imagined ordering as a conventional conceit of his age. Or we might find in it an intricate metaphor for the almost imperceptible differences that create tension, and therefore energy and movement, in even our closest relationships, a way of articulating soulfulness and physicality:

>Just such disparity
>As is 'twixt air and angels' purity,
>'Twixt women's love, and men's, will ever be.

---

[2] Katherine Rundell, *Super-Infinite: The Transformations of John Donne* (Faber, 2022)

That the poem is divided into two fourteen-line stanzas, with lines of uneven length and differing rhyme scheme, is perhaps appropriate to the complexity of Donne's argument.

In Orkney poet Edwin Muir's sonnet, 'The Confirmation' (*Collected Poems*, 1952),[3] the poet expresses a similar sense of recognition, exclaiming in the opening lines, 'Yes, yours my love is the right human face/ I in my mind had waited for this long'. Again, this Platonic sense of immanence must be brought into physical manifestation through the action of the poem, where it is the elements of the pristine natural world which might shape the metaphor by which the poet attempts to disclose and describe his love:

> what shall I call thee? A fountain in a waste,
> A well of water in a country dry
> Or anything that's honest and good, an eye
> That makes the whole world bright ...

Unlike Donne's poem the argument of the sonnet uses this sense of profound arrival and satiety to unfold an image of completeness, not to test it. However, like Donne's poem, it roots itself in beginnings and causality, where adjectives like 'primal', with its sense of primary echoed in 'first', creates a mood of both purity and potential, amplified in the soft alliteration of 'blossom' and 'blowing', which animate becoming:

> ...your open heart,
> Simple with giving, gives the primal deed,
> The first good world, the blossom, the blowing seed,

Again, we are in a heightened territory, where the 'primal deed' is love. It appropriately finds an echo in 'seed', the metaphor for its own continuous expansion and multiplication, and the images of the beloved are so integrated and harmonised with the natural world, that all its elements can be appropriated to build her physicality.

The poet realises his love through language, giving it a solidity and universality by which he can imagine it. Now she is like 'The hearth, the steadfast land, the wandering sea', images of rest, of homeliness, mixed with a sense of expansion, of swell and movement, even of restlessness. Tucked inside the image of 'the wandering sea' we can also find an image of return, where the poem comes full circle to the seeker of the earlier part of the poem, 'a traveller' who, in meeting the beloved,

---

[3] The Confirmation - National Poetry Day   Edwin Muir, Collected Poems (Faber, 1952)

> ...finds a place
> Of welcome suddenly amid the wrong
> Valleys and rock and twisting roads.

The comfortless isolation of the journey is expressed in words like 'false', 'waste country' and 'dry', as the protagonist of 'The Confirmation' wanders through a physical world empty of soul, but his search for the 'true' is connected through rhyme to the idea of 'you'. Muir's shift of tone in the sestet expands a mood of purity where 'the whole world' seems 'bright', and the echo of this phrase in 'the first good world' heightens the sense of return to unconditional love. It loops in something of the Anglo-Saxon sense of life as a journey through the harsh elemental world ('All is toilsome in the earthly kingdom'[4]), with echoes of Auden's response to that poem, 'The Wanderer' – 'ever that man goes/ Through place-keepers, through forest trees', carrying with him an image of consolation:

> There head falls forward, fatigued at evening,
> And dreams of home,
> Waving from window, spread of welcome,
> Kissing of wife under single sheet.[5]

'The Confirmation' is a poem that I often return to. As with Donne's poem, I love its opening sense of recognition, and find its apparent simplicity endearing, although its metaphors extend themselves through multiple images to create a complex and layered sense of what it means to feel completely at home with someone. Having created a whole world to serve as metaphor for the beloved, it is towards one particular quality that the poem is moving. 'The hearth, the steadfast land, the wandering sea' are 'Not beautiful or rare in every part,/ But like yourself, as they were meant to be.' Reminiscent of the final couplet of Shakespeare's Sonnet 130, 'My mistress' eyes are nothing like the sun', which parodies conventional attempts to eulogise the beloved through a naming of parts, the word 'rare' in Muir's poem resonates with a similar

---

[4] 'The Wanderer' The original Anglo-Saxon text dates from c. 900, and is by an unknown author.
[5] Auden's response, 'The Wanderer', was first published in 1930. W.H. Auden, *Collected Poems* (Faber, 1945)

energy to its Elizabethan forebear: 'And yet, by heaven, I think my love as rare/ as any she belied with false compare.'[6]

Here we have acceptance as another aspect of friendship, allowing for its imperfections. But tucked inside the word 'rare' is this idealism again, meaning both 'few in number', 'unusual', and therefore precious, but also, in an older meaning from the fifteenth century, 'airy'. We might use it in this way to describe an atmosphere as 'rarified'. Such an atmosphere is the natural home of Donne's protagonist, allowing his poem to begin with the idea of steadfastness to which Muir's poem also comes in its conclusion. In 'The Confirmation' the personification of 'the wandering sea' and 'steadfast land' give a positive agency to the forces of nature, and establish a feeling of constancy within the natural rhythms of change. For Donne the journey towards physical manifestation brings a tantalising lack of resolution, leaving us with 'Just such disparity/ As is 'twixt air and angels' purity'. A hair's breadth, perhaps, but an enlivening tension, nevertheless, between those things of differing substance, and the capturing in word, and experience, of 'Some lovely glorious nothing'.

Lesley Sharpe

---

[6] William Shakespeare, Sonnet 130

The Reading

Watch the Video

Elaine Ewart reads and discusses her poems 'Herring Girls' and 'News' which you will find on pages 8 and 9

The Alchemy Spoon
YouTube Channel

https://youtu.be/jqpDQ_mLEgg

Reviews

Diana Cant looks at two collaborations.

Sue Wallace-Shaddad & Sula Rubens
Sleeping Under Clouds
Clayhanger Press, £10.00

Vasiliki Albedo, Mary Mulholland, Simon Maddrell
All About Our Fathers
Nine Pens, £7.50

This moving book is a collaboration between the poet, Sue Wallace-Shaddad, and the painter Sula Rubens, and, having watched the on-line launch, I was struck by how much of a conversation it is – a conversation between two people with similar preoccupations expressed in different ways. The book is dedicated 'to all the children who have no choice' and focusses on the lives and plight of migrant children, represented powerfully here. Both the words and the images chart 'the backstory/ a narrative of disrupted lives.' ('Background Music')

Rubens' work is often in watercolour on old maps, which adds a fascinating depth to the images. She has used maps from an old school atlas, which means that some of the territories no longer exist. This throws up some interesting political nuances – for example, the cover picture is painted over a map of the old USSR, and Rubens has been meticulous in how she places the figures on each map. This is echoed by Wallace-Shaddad ('Traces') when she writes

> where rivers, blue-veined,
> criss-cross the skin
> of an ancient hand,

Rubens' pictures are peopled by children – often sibling groups, but with very few parental figures. Instead, there are goats and their kids, and geese – all potential companions, but also sources of livelihood and food in an uncertain world. As the accompanying words ask – 'will they be kept until old age?' ('Grounded'). We are drawn into the images, not only by the very direct gaze of the children, but also by our desire to read the maps, to try and plot their unfathomable journeys. The sea becomes a particularly potent symbol, reminding us of the fate of so many migrants, and especially of the photograph of the drowned Syrian/Kurdish child that moved so many, and was especially resonant for both of these authors.

Wallace-Shaddad's poems are correspondingly simple, direct and, for the most part, relatively unadorned. She describes what she sees, in a spare and straightforward way that mirrors the life of these impoverished children, living in a harsh and unforgiving landscape. But there are also elements of playfulness, when the children long for an old tyre to become a swing, to play football or to rest on an abandoned sofa: 'How many children have pummelled the stuffing,/ jumped, pillow-fought, feathers flying? ('On the Sofa').

The poems serve the pictures well – they draw attention to detail, ask important questions and amplify the realities of a life on the move, without sentimentalising or catastrophising – we are left to do our own thinking.

A final word about this book as an object in its own right – it is very beautiful. The shape, form and typesetting really do the pictures and words justice – simple, arresting and powerful. One to treasure and revisit.

༺༻

This collection of poems, part of Nine Pens 'Nine Series Anthologies', is a companion piece to the earlier *All About Our Mothers*, by the same authors. All three poets take nine poems each to address their fathers, and the result is a fascinating poetic exploration of paternal legacy, though we need to remember this is poetry, not autobiography.

Although all three poets have a distinctive style and voice, there are striking similarities to their memories of their fathers. Fathers could do with a bit of rehabilitation in the poetic world, and yet what comes across most powerfully is the ambivalence evident in these poems. Fathers are frequently objects of fear, allied to undercurrents of violence or abuse. Images of guns reoccur, scenes of conflict, together with moments of unspoken tenderness and care. As Albedo ('Landowner') puts it:

> Sending me flowers
> with the right hand, while your left
> is over my mouth.

And then there is the task of caring for an ailing father, with all the complex feelings that brings, as in Mulholland's 'Letting go':

> I don't know why he used to frighten me.
> These days he's a child I don't want to have
> to look after.

Albedo's father can be a frightening figure too, variously a scholar, a liar and a bully; full of charismatic menace but also a powerful dream figure, defining the internal emotional landscape. There are memorable phrases – 'rain percussing/the roof', 'a cigar tamponing his lips'; and some arresting line breaks that give these poems movement and strength. She has an unerring eye for detail – for example, as her father blows out candles at his eightieth birthday ('Carnivore'): 'the cake untouched/glossy with spit and cherries…./a small mercy of greens for me.'

We learn that Mulholland's father was an army man, and images of conflict, war, and weapons are mirrored on the domestic scale by references to plucking and gutting partridges and fly fishing. The prose poem 'Feast' is a meticulous description of preparing pheasants, and of the small child's instinctive and symbolic revulsion – 'So small. So bruised.' In 'Our silent years', the child's memories are of a different war:

>It's always about taking sides.
>
>Now I see it was never my war with you.
>When I was a child we lived in a divided country.

And the final poem in this section, 'Letting go', returns to the idea of ambivalence with a searing honesty, as Mulholland describes visiting her father in hospital:

>I speak across him, *I can't*
>*understand why he's holding on –*
>*as if he's forgotten to go.*
>The nurse says, *you know he's listening.*
>I knew he was listening.

Simon Maddrell, the final of the three poets, opens his selection by setting down something unforgettable in 'Gripping', where the implications of abuse hang in the air. But again, things are not clear-cut; there are descriptions of the delights of picking fruit in 'Whinberry Pie':

>it was the autumn of our content
>>despite those things that were not,
>
>it was the season of crumbles
>>fed by blushed Bramleys
>
>and every black hedgerow we could find.

This is a single father who, as well as being frightening, sets about sewing the number 9 on his son's football shirt, and is delighted by his subsequent goal. The long poem, 'God didn't create anything', deals with the father's imagined responses to his son's queerness, and the father's own cancer, structured around eleven stanzas referencing a different type of therapy. The irregularly repeated refrain lines – 'with his pulpit certainty'; 'in this world without a cure'; 'there's no need for that anymore', create a tension between progression and regression that serves the subject matter well.

All of these poets have spoken about the joy of collaborating on this project, and the resonances and cross-fertilisation that have occurred as a result. If you haven't already, I would strongly recommend reading this anthology in tandem with the 'Mothers' issue, and congratulations are due to Nine Pens for this creative series.

Diana Cant

Wendy Kyle looks at a debut collection that delivers an Ars Poetica for expressions of 'madness', through the eye of Hurricane Maria and the fictional characters of Dominican-born Jean Rhys.

Celia A Sorhaindo
Radical Normalisation
Carcanet Poetry, £11.99

In her debut collection, *Radical Normalisation*, Sorhaindo spotlights marginalised voices of 'madness' in a world where trauma strikes like a hurricane. Our recent experiences of pandemic, forest fires, flooding and isolation have an almost biblical resonance.

These poems come as a timely challenge to our attitudes about mental health as natural disaster becomes an undeniable component of the human experience. The meaning of normality, for Sorhaindo, needs radical revision to incorporate compassion for behaviours of despair that impose altered states of being.

The conceptual expansion of madness and recovery is intended to counter the reductive dehumanisation of people with mental health disorders. Sorhaindo's Ars Poetica produces a kind of creative survivalism, including the mystical and Shamanistic healing in her poetic space.

In the poem 'Joining Dots is Radically Normal', the speaker refers to herself as 'unhinged' yet also a 'straightforward poet', thus normalising her experience. Her poetic voices speak from different realities where 'surreal visionary/symbols', 'totems and talismans', even Voodoo may offer imaginative relief to a disordered mind. Here, poetic craft is re-imagined as a supernatural force like 'linked Ouija board/hands'.

Sorhaindo uses the 2017 Hurricane Maria in Dominica as a metaphor for the overpowering terror of the individual obliteration and tragedy of human disconnection. Recovery comes only from collective experience, revealing an urgent change from individualism. Thus the hurricane becomes a communal trauma, imagined as a powerful necessity that will shake us to the bones and awaken us to one another.

The hurricane also represents the speaker's desire for cultural belonging and the sharing of intergenerational survival of psychotrauma. Ancestral narratives of slavery, colonialism and natural disaster in Dominica connect an individualised self to a deeper identity, harder to uproot. She wants connection; to 'magic my future ancestral gods' ('Joining Dots…'). She believes that the poem can draw in the alienated from damaging human exiles, 'in cutting silence i too heard the community/of madness that i am and/I know now, I | belong| be al (one)| here'. ('erasure drawn…sketched out').

This collection has an intertextual connectivity with Dominican-born writer Jean Rhys, whose fictional characters explore notions of female madness and ancestral trauma. Sorhaindo's 'doh let me be lonely' is a mother's dramatic monologue made poignantly intimate in Caribbean register. The form – a breathless prose poem – creates a desperate tempo, like a last calling out to her son. We see her as she unravels into the insanity of loneliness.

In reference to Rhys' *Wide Sargasso Sea*, the madwoman's memories are scrambled confusedly through time, intensifying her severance from present-tense reality. While Sorhaindo's speaker is certain that 'if dey ketch me dey skin me alive', she cares only for human connection: 'son, son, why yuh stay away so long? i feel a dark hollow/ in mi insides an around mi outside head. an empty empty.'

This collection also narrows its lens to the intimate and familial with poems showing specific histories of pain and fierce cultural loyalty to ancestral courage. 'In the Air', the speaker displays pride at their grandmother's endurance, 'her knees raw with prayer', during the hurricane and her 'words gone as wounds appeared. /She walked on water'.

In their 'mother's debris garden', the narrator contemplates women in her family who survived brutal experiences. These poems are like treasures from a family album. In 'My Sister and I Are Picking Mangoes', normal domesticity surfaces with tenderness in the collapsed aftermath of devastation – even though nothing is normal at all. What they treasure after loss is renewal of the shared natural world, where a 'beloved mango tree is recovery', taking on familial status.

The collection continues to circle back to compassion for those who lose mental stability, with a rethink of what healing means:

I know what it's

like to fall, bruise, split skin & expose flesh all the way
down to bone-white seed, so I pull down & catch; save
some mangoes from this fate.

For Sorhaindo, it is time for the 'crazy' I/eye to have its space in contemporary lyric address. She insists the white space of her poems are a centre of cultural significance – an artistic necessity for social transformation. Her exacting use of negative space, tabulation and punctuation use black marks on white space like a precision tool for cutting the pain of a speaker into the page. In 'Dead Poets, Prophets &

Bob Marley' her poem aspires for the colloquy of her cultural prophets and yet exhibits an anxiety to protect them from being 'garrotted with our own /chain of thought'. Even the use of a colon becomes significant like a sentry overlooking the start of a line – possessive of the artist's words:

> What if we dare
> to be heard?
> : Given enough air
> waves for poetry and reggae strong
> and true enough to free — words to hang on

In her opening poem, 'Poetic Turn of Events', Sorhaindo seems to be reminding herself of the responsibility to maintain The Poem as a communal radical to mindfully normalise others 'who fell off the edge' ('Crucible').

> The Poets do not know what to make
> of it all, at all, at all! The People are
> asking the Poets to listen; hear & read
> them for a change. I know! Crazy, right?

This powerful collection seems to encompass a desire for a more radical schematic for poetry: that people become their own poets and prophets in a collective space rather than worsening the disconnect between Poets and People.

Wendy Kyle

Julian Bishop looks at three new collections which offer very different perspectives on relationships and the natural world.

L Kiew
More Than Weeds
Nine Arches Press, £10.99

Jorie Graham
To 2040
Carcanet, £15.99

Vanessa Lampert
Say It With Me
Seren, £9.99

According to the Oxford Dictionary, a weed is *a wild plant growing where it is not wanted and in competition with cultivated plants.* L Kiew's first collection *More Than Weeds* takes this definition and applies it to migration, or, as she puts it in 'Corydalis lutea' (aka fumewort):

> When she has a wasp in her mouth
> she asks: can weed be just another
> name the rain calls down
> for refugee, unforced flower.

But the '*where it is not wanted*' part of the definition is the presiding part of this metaphor, many of the poems using specific weeds to explore related themes of dislocation and alienation.

Kiew skilfully weaves her own experience into the mix on both political and personal levels, with some poems combining the two. In 'Splits and rasps', where *rasps* could be noun or verb, her 'tongue tills the earth':

> Culvert. Tongue trying, overspills. Damn
> my teeth. Tongue held back. Tongue released
> a crop. Spitting out. Being spat out.
> Being spat on. Lips missed, spot on.

As Kiew explains in the 'Seeding and sproutings' notes section at the back of the book, she flips between English and Teochew, the Southern Min language spoken in the Chaoshan region of eastern Guangdong. Language itself becomes another means of othering in poems like 'Buddleja davidii' where the plant (butterfly bush) opens the poem by asking '*What is my own   name?'* but triumphantly concludes by growing into 'bees' amah shrub   vigorous I own and/ am arching   I name myself   perfect'.

This and some of the more political poems excoriate the role of those who not so long ago were grandly described as plant hunters, who lent their names to many garden plants. *Buddleja davidii* is named after a French missionary who 'collected' specimens in China for despatch back to Paris. Others such as Robert Fortune ignored local laws and basically smuggled plants such as tea out of China. Kiew employs the plants to deliver a dramatic monologue which lambasts Fortune and his entitled ilk as 'zealous collectors of scant morality' but again the poem strikes a triumphant note by the end:

> hearts here are
> groundswelled flowers flowers
> flowers from bulbs and shoots
> emerging shy saplings heal
> disturbance of earth spadebroken
> calm is the foliage
> beyond threat of hand axe mower
> and we grow

Similarly 'Wisteria' explores how seedlings were 'transported' back to the UK by John Reeves, Chief Inspector of Tea at Canton, as cuttings from a plant growing in the garden of a Chinese colleague in Canton which the poet describes as 'a stealing a separating', presumably a reference to the East India Company which subjugated and plundered vast tracts of south Asia. The poem ends with the ironic line 'I count each cutting'.

Quite a few poems in the collection offer a variation on this theme (e.g. 'Karwinski's fleabane', 'Impatiens glandulifera'), the latter mourning 'our mown sisters/ not allowed forgiveness'. Others strike a more personal, even erotic note such as 'Boscage', a succulent title in itself. I'm not sure about the unsubtle 'topiary balls, viridescent and rustling' but the poem goes on:

> His hands part low branches, spread twigs, show me
> the hungrier of heart, their furred wriggling;
> so many caterpillars are stripping
> green tissue, denuding stems.

This tangled verdancy extends to language as well in 'Underground' where with each word 'a leaf tilts to listen' and 'Forest *text*', a clever bifold form where the writing process becomes synonymous with plant growth:

> leaves through which *eyes and claws*
> shoots and signs erupt *shape scrape*
> word interrupt bark *and musang tails*
> branches logograph *ideograms of fur*
> in arching liernes *lagomorphs and*
> foliole accumulate *tupai scat signs*

And naturally (excuse the pun) for a collection that majors on very much contemporary concerns there are poems that look forward to the impact of climate change. In 'Geoxyle',

> Words spark the silence
> yet nothing's been said
> about the sun's smother,
> its hardening spread.

The poem describes Earth blackening and concludes fatalistically 'what happens / is what happens.' However, the collection ends on a note of defiance with the poet telling us although she has flung herself 'into the conflagration' she 'longs to live. Here.'

―――――

Which is a sentiment shared – with similar equivocation – by Jorie Graham's *To 2040*. The collection opens with the words 'Are we/ extinct yet', the first two words as the title of the poem, a question (without a question mark) addressed by most of the poems that follow where the voice switches unnervingly between a human world and one presided over by drones, AI and VR, as in the title poem:

> With whom am I speaking, are you one or many, what are u, are u, do I make my- self clear, is this which we called speech what u use, are u a living form such as the form I inhabit now letting it speak me.

As with so much of Graham's work, the underlying concern is with how to deal with a 'now' teetering on a tightrope between a natural world that increasingly only belongs to the past and a potentially apocalyptic future, where memory is at best unreliable and hope far from a guarantee. As she asked in her poem 'The Post Human' (in her previous collection *Fast*): 'Now. Is that a place now. Do you have a now.'

To 2040 picks up from this point, for example in the poem 'Dis' which is set in a hospital where 'I can't /remember why it is we /love' where a crow appears as a kind of shamanic presence or maybe visitor from the past and

> it just peers &
> overgrows me with layers of
> glances, till I'm bodied again,
> till I'm thick, & it's saying
> you are in history dear child
>
> you are only in history,
>
> you are not in time,
> & you're not getting
> out.

Later it's a woodpecker (in 'Day') that arrives and opens up 'the hole/ in my heart' to rebuke the poet: 'You had a lifetime/ to get this story,/ to write its long and bitter poem.'

Similarly in the title poem she questions the concept of time – particularly in the sense of having enough time – itself. The book uses a futuristic lens to ask whether we – or more specifically the poet – are making the best use of how they record the moment:

> Years pulled their lengths through us like long wet strings, and we hung onto them, they strung us a ways along, & up, they kept us from drowning in the terrible minutes.

Unlike other poems in the volume, the title poem sprawls across and fills the page, which like many of Graham's poems makes it difficult to digest given the constant shifts of thought process:

> Place as much as you can in your heart. It doesn't matter what's in your mind. When you come here all you will be left w/is a heart they spill out, a tin cup, they count up what you put in it, they shake it into a small burlap sack, they weigh it, they tie it up, they do not give it back. It is then you are placed at your window to watch. Then the snow begins.

Who is the 'they' performing this butchery on the human heart? The suggestion is of an AI run wild, an artificial world where the 'flawless birds' are 'wired to perfection' to sing. Hence Graham's vision of 2040 is one of desperate uncertainty and regret for opportunities missed, what she later calls 'the dune of the future' where nothing can be taken at face value even if it presents as such – hence perhaps the deliberate lack of question marks after an interrogative statement. And double-meanings abound, the poem 'I Am Still' begins:

> on the earth.
> My interval
> is fixed. Who
> fixed it.
>
> For a while
> all that came out
> was answers.
> Then nothing.

Only the 'interval' is fixed, whatever that may be – life? The line in the poem? What happens when the answers are obvious but aren't addressed? The poem looks to 'wind or light' to guide her, even 'spells', but in it she fears even the air will become 'unbreathable', a prophetic line realised this last summer in a New York blanketed by smoke from Canadian wildfires. The poem concludes tellingly 'How could we/ not have heard'.

In past collections Graham has disrupted form and syntax, deploying (irritatingly at times, I think) chevrons to suggest urgency or right-justifying poems so they bump up against the margins of a page. Here she drops vowels, e.g. 'sd' instead of 'said', while personal pronouns get contracted in lines like 'you close yr eyes/ for clues, u peer, inhale, listen madly for clues' which adds to the discombobulating effect of the entire collection.

As ever, the more successful poems for me are strongly image-driven rather than just conceptual, be they 'The Vase of Quince Branches You Sent Me' or 'In Reality', the latter using the potentially clichéd river of life in a fresh way, if 'fresh' is the right word for water suffused with 'benzenes… foams made of monies' and 'the silt everywhere widens' until

> The water is down to a handful of jewels
> tossed out here and there on the miles of dry sand.
> That's all I recall.

> Then the keel hits and I'm tipped over gently,
> as if to be fully & finally
> poured out.

Of course the poem concludes with an image of 'open sea' (which was disappointingly predictable) but at least offers a glimpse of hope in a future of 'broken furniture' and 'abandoned shops' where if nothing else 'the spider is still here'.

The collection ends on a hint of redemption. The prospect of a sun 'toughing everything less and less tenderly' is replaced by one where:

> out of the touching of one atom by an
> other, out of the
> accident of
> touch, the rain
> came.

Graham claims she takes speaking the past to the future to be 'a primary moral responsibility of the art' and it wouldn't be stretching the point to read this collection as a manifesto and demonstration of exactly that.

※

If you want clues about how to write poems that win competitions, you might well consider studying Vanessa Lampert's debut collection *Say It With Me*. The notes at the back reference more than a couple of dozen winners in just three years. Clearly these poems hit the right spot for the judges. A recent graduate of the Poetry School MA course, she's very technically adept, but fortunately the collection reads nothing like a series of coursework exercises responding to prompts, which must be a hazard to negotiate when choosing poems for any collection post-graduation.

So what are the themes Lampert explores so successfully? Think of a reckoning with the past, be it in the form of forgiveness, acceptance or simply nostalgia. Think of family relationships, from the ecstatic (as in 'Our Song', where the singer wears 'sapphires and diamonds/ in rows at her throat') to the tragic – poems about a brother who took his life threaded through the collection.

And mix in attempts to hold all this together without toppling over like the sandcastles that feature in a couple of poems. In these poems there's always a sense that the tide is in danger of coming in – or already has – and washing something precious away. In 'Sand', which takes place during childhood on Woolacombe beach, she reflects:

> In a few weeks my parents will separate,
> but now our orange windbreak holds them
>   close together in flowery beach chairs
>
> safe from the wind.

Many poems seek to find shelter behind that windbreak which sometimes becomes the speaker herself, as in the only slightly ironic 'Happy Family Soliloquy':

> Conflict? I survive it, I'm hell-bent
> on healing every rift. Love's certainty
> will always wait for me. People.
> More than the world, they want to live in me,
> seek a swift departure from the shambles
> of before.

The self-assured tone of this poem has a slight head-girlishness about it ('Little wonder that more than the world/ they want to live in me') which is picked up in other poems such as 'Duty' where she reflects on her time as school Locust Monitor 'maybe I was born for this' which concludes 'no locust ate another on my watch'. I bet!

But this never translates into prissiness. Far from it, in fact. Lampert is a master at wrong-footing the reader, as in the unpromisingly titled 'Birthday Magic' which is about two girls filling up balloons and pretending they're babies. Oh dear, I thought… but then:

> Mel looks at me and says
> *let's do it!* and we throw our babies as hard as we can
> against the wall and watch them explode.
> We laugh at the sound of it, at the two whopping
> wet stains on the brick and the small scraps
> of pink rubber lying on the patio

In other poems though, the past is viewed through the lens of regret. 'Snow' begins 'Just as I start becoming a more decent person/ a past unkindness will fall, silent as snow'. The poem explores how an act of meanness against two girls was thrown into sharp relief when their home burned down, 'snow in their hair/ while the windows glowed fierce orange'. This illustrates Lampert's skill at making an image work hard on several levels, be it to suggest silence, coldness or the act of unkindness itself.

In 'Wimbledon 2020' the past is actively manipulated. The poem opens:

> I'm changing what happened.
> In the new truth, my dad did not die young.
> He's out on the street in front of his house
> with his old man's face lifted
> to a cloudless sky, brilliant summer.

Here the sky is the presiding image in the poem, where later on a trapped bird will be released from being stuck in an a roof space. A reaching towards a better future underpins other poems more explicitly, especially some of the more personal poems like 'Some Pleasures', a list poem which celebrates all kinds of small pleasures from Radiohead songs to couscous and ends: 'Opening the window of a train/ as it speeds through open countryside, taking off/ my platinum wedding ring. Throwing it.'

You'll notice another strength of the collection here, the unpredictable line break. Very few poems misfire although I wasn't entirely convinced by the end of 'Say It, Hiker', another 'freedom' poem, which concludes with an image of 'the constant tide/ turning. Keeping its hold on the light.'

The final poem in the collection, 'End Party', ends more simply and strikes a more convincing note. The poet reflects:

> It's been so long since the sky
> took anything I was ready
> to surrender.
>
> Let's pen new hopes on a label
> and make ourselves
> an occasion up there.
> Nothing fancy, champagne
> and a pink sunset,
> no-one else, only us
>
> watching two balloons
> lean to the whim
> of the wind.

Julian Bishop

SK Grout reviews two collections that navigate overcoming adversity, the body and the systems of power that surround us.

Monica Youn
From From
Carcanet Press, £14.99

Katie Farris
Standing in the Forest of Being Alive
Pavilion Poetry, £8.80

'Whiteness is the privilege of not being contained in that way. I wanted the audience to be unsettled by this first poem. To say, you're not going to get to just sit here and happily consume exotic stories. That's not what this book is going to be. I want to make you uncomfortable. I want you to be questioning your consumption of what you're reading, to understand how that implicates you and implicates me.'[7]

From From is celebrated US poet Monica Youn's first collection to be published in the UK (her fourth in the US). The title is a play on the micro aggressive question, 'But where are you really from?' And, as she reflects in the quote above, it's a forensic and unflinching approach to structures of power, particularly race and racial privilege. How do we relate and interact with these structures, specifically racism and misogyny, and what do these relationships look like – for example, in a schoolyard, in a neighbourhood street, in a corner store? And zooming out on a grander scale, how does racism manifest and reproduce in the shape of the stories our communities share – in myth, parable, the storytelling of history? What are the spaces, and the distances, between each other, especially if racism begins as the constructed act of putting someone into a container?

The poems are divided into five sections broadly engaging with Greek myth ('Asia Minor'); eight poems considering growing up ('Deracinations'); poems considering the broader context of society ('Western Civ'); parables ('The Magpies'); a long diary/essay section reflecting on the pandemic and the rise of anti-Asian attacks in the US during the same time ('In the Passive Voice'). This last section traverses topics such as art, nature, the 1992 Los Angeles uprising and the murder of black teenager, Latasha Harlins, by a Korean-American shopkeeper, Du Soon Ja. The collection opens and closes with two long poems, 'Study of Two Figures (Pasiphaë/Sado)' and 'Detail of the Rice Chest', that act

---

[7] Monica Youn, from an interview with Dorothy Wang, BOMB Magazine, Winter 2023

as doubles, in the titles and poems, and for each other – a kind of opening and closing door to the collection. Doubles, as a further deepening of an engagement with space, community, and identity, appear not just in the title but throughout the collection – 'Parable of the Magpie and the Mirror', 'Study of Two Figures (Ignatz/Krazy)', 'Rejected. Ejected' (from 'In the Passive Voice'.)

So much acts as window and mirror in each poem. They are told in a direct style and presented as a kind of conversation, driven by tone. 'And the magpie flew west and came to a land where there were many flocks and herds that were ill-tended and diseased.' ('Parable of the Magpies in the West') and 'We're hardwired to draw lines around pieces of experience.' ('In the Passive Voice'). Youn allows the parable and myth poems to feel both urgent and prescient, without overwhelming. Greek myths have long been an interest for Youn, but she uses them to consider the broader structures of power and racism – if the Ancient Greeks talked about otherness, what did that look like and why was it predominantly Asian? Poems that consider structures of power apply questions that are nuanced and not static. Youn asks, what are the poetics of difference versus the poetics of authenticity? 'I know who Prince Sado is, I can read the Hangul word *Sado*. But I do not speak Korean.' ('Detail of the Rice Chest'). How does a poet write about the traumas and vulnerabilities of their community within the broader contexts of power, racism, and capitalism; what is erased when one community is elevated above others? From 'In the Passive Voice':

Today I get a message from my Brooklyn apartment building listserv. An Asian-American woman says she was accosted by an anti-Asian harasser while fumbling with her key trying to enter the building. […] I draft an email in reply, urging residents not to call the police, who will only worsen the situation, who might prevent unhoused neighbors from accessing the nearby services they need.

Each section, each poem, each word and line are deeply considered; much time and thought has been spent developing the collection from the tone, structure, voice and rhythm, the context and content of each poem, as well as the repetition and recurring images and extended metaphors circling back through poems and sections. Just as Youn has spent prodigious time crafting these poems, ('Thank you to my fellow members of the Racial Imaginary Institute for their deep influence on my thinking about race and artmaking', from 'Acknowledgements') so, too, time spent reading and re-reading this collection rewards the audience. The final poem is the kind of poem that lives and breathes in my memory. In many ways, this review will fall short because of the complexity of *From From*. (I encourage readers to seek out interviews with Youn – for example, with David Naimon at Tin House, with Dorothy Wang at *BOMB Magazine* and her online launch Q&A with Sarah Howe – which further exemplify her deep dedication to critical thinking.) It is a collection that asks complicated questions about how the applications of art and creative practice manifest in real world community-building and demand lengthy consideration of the ways in which we interact with each other, navigating privileges and systems of power.

☙❧

Emily Dickinson, famously, wrote: 'hope is a thing with feathers'. As she noted in one of her letters, 'My birds fly far off, nobody knows where they go to, but you see I know they are coming back, and other people don't, that makes the difference'[8]. Despite their struggle with physical and psychological pain and the difficulty and absurdity of cancer, Katie Farris' poems return, as 'Outside Atlanta Cancer Care' states, over and over 'to this point of wonder'. In other words, the collection makes its centrepoint the search for hope despite overwhelming adversity.

Standing in the Forest of Being Alive is Farris' debut collection, published in the US with Alice James Books and in the UK with Pavilion Poetry. 'Tell It Slant', contrary to its jaunty title, tells us directly and straightforwardly Farris' diagnosis of breast cancer aged thirty-six:

> a stranger called and said,
> *You have cancer. Unfortunately.*
> And then hung up the phone.

But as Farris has stated, 'One of the goals of my book is to demystify the experience of cancer, opening up the conversation, and letting people know that it comes with its horrors, but also, in a strange way, with its delights.'[9] As the opening poem's title 'Why Write Poetry in a Burning World' leads into its first two lines, 'To train myself to find in the midst of hell / what isn't hell.'

There are three major threads running through the collection: cancer poems, America poems and love poems (with some poems preoccupied with all three). We traverse a personal and political timeline

---

[8] Emily Dickinson, from a letter to Sophia Holland, written *c.* March, 1859
[9] 'Katie Farris Battles Cancer and Insurrections with Poetic Humor and Hope in *Standing in the Forest of Being Alive*', interview with James Morehead, Viewless Wings Poetry Podcast

encountering cancer diagnosis and treatment, doctor and hospital appointments, at the same time as America is erupting with protest, political unrest and navigating a global pandemic. 'Five Days Before the Mastectomy, Insurrection at the Capitol'. The love poems are directed both to a lover, but also to a love of poetry; Emily Dickinson is a major figure in these pages as a recurring character, from 'A Row of Rows'

> And was Whitman
> or Dickinson the greater
> epic poet?

and as a source of inspiration: 'Emiloma: A Riddle & An Answer' employs the rhyme and rhythm of Dickinson, and 'Outside Atlanta Cancer Care' her famous dashes and curious questions. These poems are coy and sexy, work as memoir and lyric, engage rhyme and rhythm, insulate within the poetic world and engage outside with nature. They are funny, too. From 'An Unexpected Turn of Events Midway Through Chemotherapy'

> I'd like some sex please.
> I'm not too picky -
>   (after all, have you seen me?

The collection is rich in variety in form and poem length – there are shorter poems displayed on half a page and several haiku. These act as a kind of buffer between longer, more contextually challenging poems such as 'The Invention of America' or 'Ode to Money, or Patient Appealing Health Insurance for Denial of Coverage' – two poems that place the ramifications of political decisions within the personal sphere. Farris has also talked about finding the rhythm of the poems within a body: 'This shorter style, combined with writing love poems, led me to adopt a two-beat-per-line meter, which I thought of as two heartbeats together in a line. Dickinson's alternating three- and four-beat lines also influenced my work, as I mostly write in iambic pentameter.'[10] Rather than break the poems into sections about each of her themes, Farris weaves these narratives throughout the collection, waxing and waning in length and conversation, as if to suggest that just as there will be bad days, there will be good days too. Days where you can consider, from 'What Would Root'

---

[10] Ibid.

> It was May,
> it was May, it was May, and the air was sweet
> with pine and island mountain lilac.

One of the standout poems for me that navigated all three of her themes is 'To the Pathologist Reading My Breast, Palimpsest'. Written with Kimberley Point du Jour MD, this poem creates a layering of the language of medicine with the language of poetry, across the body of the speaker. 'To rhyme *mastectomy*, I thought my dear friend's pregnancy'. This poem highlights the way language can uplift and, inversely, can dehumanise, how we must navigate words we are unfamiliar with and how we are comfortable with words we use every day. As a kind of hermit crab poem, the poet is trying and struggling to find a home within this strange and alienating language; that language, and poetry, is both an act of creation, and a breaking down; to make something new of the diagnosis; to find a path forward to hope.

SK Grout

Sue Wallace-Shaddad looks at a collection and a pamphlet which have family at their heart

Latch
Rebecca Goss
Carcanet, £12.99

Jill Abram
Forgetting My Father
Broken Sleep Books, £8.50

The door latch is open on the cover of Goss's new collection, *Latch*, inviting us into her poetry. She writes about returning to where she grew up in Suffolk but also suggests that county, with its 'stuff of spells' and 'freedoms of a wood' as described in 'Arger Fen', has shaped her relationships with her daughter, husband, siblings and parents.

The collection opens with 'The Hounds' which sets the poems within the context of the countryside with its very different sounds to the city: 'Their lament/ rising across fields'. The visceral nature of howling is captured in 'O this night, this bidding,/ claws at the latch'. There is a hint of nostalgia and magic in Goss's description of where she grew up in 'The Farm': 'Semi-derelict, ramshackle whimsy of a place'. She packs this poem with detail: '[...] Cats who never came indoors. Fifty hens./ Dog roaming for bitches'. In 'Woman Returns to Childhood Home, Finds Herself Amongst Others', the speaker weaves memories of her parents, as if apparitions, into the present, when she visits the farm:

> You're narrating thirteen years here,
> cat stepping casually over our cake
> when I notice my mother behind you,

The reader is conscious of the passage of time throughout this collection. 'Bricks' is an eloquent poem about the house Goss now lives in and how her daughter moves through the house: 'each crooked portal taking her/ to another ancient part'. Goss suggests the bricks will form a record of where 'my daughter's weight made history'. In the poem 'What Will It Be Like To Be Here?' she considers how her growing daughter might feel about this place. Her daughter might

> hate it here,
> for its oldness, everything
> it lacks. And I will love it
> for the years it gave me

Goss often uses the past to help her navigate the present. She remembers when she walked 'the pitch-black mile' back from the pub with teenage girlfriends in the poem 'When It Feels Hot, That Rage Against Me'. She concludes, when it comes to her daughter's life, she will understand 'your need to be away from me and with girls'.

'The Pact' is a powerful poem of sibling experience, of a secret kept 'held far into our adult lives'. The youngest boy falls from a height between 'blocks, barn-stacked, almost to the roof, forbidden.' The poet builds a sense of panic with long narrative sentences. One of the aspects of Goss's childhood that comes across here, and also in the poem 'Cousins', is the way the young have a strong sense of tribe. The poet seems to wish the next generation to have this closeness: 'They were meant to know each other/ in this piece of countryside.'

The collection features age-old features and traditions of the countryside, local bird and animal life, stubble burning and the perils facing children. The poem 'In Song Flight', written in couplets, creates a feeling of space and height, reminding the reader of the particular flight of the skylark which is a 'Sky Shepherd,/ watching me in barley'. In 'Pheasant in Rear-View Mirror', there is a beautiful image of the pheasant: 'its iridescence/ a failing flare in the meadow.' At the end of the poem, the child almost seems to become a bird: 'your body appearing/ and vanishing in succession'. The poem 'We Saw Deer' unfolds in slow motion, each tercet presenting one facet of the encounter: '[…] her deliberate pause/ to look back at us, the quiet muscle of her'.

An interesting aspect of the collection is the detailed focus on the skills of those who work in the countryside. In 'Blacksmith, Making', the choice of words and visual image makes for a striking opening:

> I met a man fluent
> in the lexicon of spark
> and watched him stand, forge-lit,

The ancient skill of lime-plastering is described in 'Close Work' with simple onomatopoeic words, often derived from old English: 'ring shank nail' and 'place, gauge, pin, knock'. 'We Are Buried Under Lime', a poem about burying mementos in the walls of the house, includes mention of 'The craftsmen who paused their tools/ to add their trade and autograph.' There are echoes of Goss' past before her return to Suffolk and the loss of her first daughter Ella, which she wrote about in her collection 'Her Birth'. Goss acknowledges 'death/ is something we are well versed in' in 'Deathwatch Beetles'. However, she finds that the countryside tempers pain in 'Under a New Sky': 'grief diminishes/ to a more manageable form.' The poem 'Nest' includes the poignant lines:

> […] and all mothers
> who lay their babies down, knowing
> they cannot stay beside them.'

Goss has said that 'Stars in a Field' is the only poem she wrote specifically for her husband in the collection. Suffolk comes across as a place of refuge: 'I have asked for this county/ to soften in you'. She wishes

> salt in our kisses
> close a cottage door
>
> stay with me behind it

The collection is dedicated to Goss's parents and their apparent story also runs through the poems. 'There Was a Swing' imagines the parents meeting as teenagers: 'They danced most of the night/ this girl, this boy'. In 'Pictures of You', the mother (who also appears to be shown in a photograph at the end of the book), is depicted in the lines: 'the red hair he loves/ blown across your forehead'.

Latch repays several re-readings. The intertwining of themes, memory and the fluidity of time makes for a very evocative collection steeped in a personal discovery of what it means to both re-live and create a sense of home.

❧

The dedication to Jill Abram's father Leo Abram, *Loved and Missed*, at the front of the pamphlet sums up its emotional heart. There is an irony in the title as it suggests forgetting, but the act of writing this pamphlet is one of remembrance.

Abram sets the context with poems about childhood and other members of the family before focusing on the father. She adds Jewish words 'mezzuzah' and 'shul' in 'We Used The Back Door' when describing a childhood neighbour. The first two poems describe the challenges of being Jewish. In 'Like a Fiddler on the Roof', Abram describes 'a colourful straggle/ walking through Hungary'. In 'How to Belong', she writes that teenagers 'At Jewish youth club' were 'lured' by 'The Evangelicals' and 'They wanted all of us.'

Abram uses fine detail to great effect in many of the poems. In 'Inheritance', we learn of her grandmother's legacy: 'A coat, a jacket, five pairs of knickers and Alfred'. Alfred is a bronze tortoise. Abram has a bittersweet sense of humour which emerges repeatedly. In 'At My Mother's Knee', the speaker recounts 'My bike came ready-rusted, our piano was second hand,/ only cheap brands in our house, no state-of-the-art for us'. She creates a sequence of short definitions describing the speaker's sister in 'My Sister is'. In each case, there is a title, for example: 'a gold coin' or 'a steamroller'. She sets up an expectation, then comments upon it, as in 'a window': 'Round, square or arched/ Hmm, certainly arch'. Unexpectedly, the final definition of the sister is as 'a coffin' 'Made to measure, lined with silk' – I read this as the sister having the last word.

Abram's father's life, illness and death are revealed in a series of poignant poems. 'Slow Orphaning' is particularly devastating:

> A heart attack slowed him. A bypass stopped him
> at a stroke. His body survived fifteen years
> while his mind died and I grieved for
> so long […]

In the poem 'Leaving', she describes the way the father no longer remembers visits and how

> he held my finger in a baby-strong grip,
> so I couldn't leave, smiled with his whole face
> so I wouldn't leave […]

The final lines may have particular resonance for anyone caring for a loved one: 'I wish away the time till his supper is served/ so I can leave without a leave-taking.' In 'Many Happy Returns', the family come to visit on Leo's 87th birthday. The structure of this poem, with its two columns of questions and answers, mirrors the disconnect of memory. I enjoyed the humour of the last line: 'I'm 87. I'd better sit down'. In 'Marriage Vow', the reader is given a glimpse of happier times, when the father and mother met: 'Mum says Dad was brought as a date for her sister/ by his friend who said, *This is my friend Leo*'. The poem ends sadly: 'Mum says *We've had the better, now's the worse.*' 'I Have Forgotten My Father' is a key poem in the pamphlet, with five sextets full of detailed reminiscences about the father's life. The poem clearly shows someone *'loved and missed':* 'how he made me feel grown up by asking me to choose/ his ties, making me his golf caddy […]'

Abram's pamphlet is a warm and loving testament to her father with poems informed by the distillation of memory and the act of caring over a long period of time. The pamphlet gains power from that.

Sue Wallace-Shaddad

Reviews in Brief

Zoë Walkington
I Hate to Be the One to Tell You This
smith|doorstop, £6

This pamphlet is hilarious, and not least because its humour is uncomfortably rooted in situations a decimal point away from domestic possibilities. In 'Decimal point' the narrator accidentally pays £3750 (presumably instead of £37.50) and pictures the milkman 'in his milk float/ straight to Thomas Cook/ to book his trip to Mexico'. In 'Imagine', the narrator addresses a husband bringing 'your mistress home to meet the family' and his wife's 'mouth which for three years you have only seen as a line/ hangs open in a soft O'.

Zoë Walkington was a winner in the PBS competition 2022, is professor of psychology at the Open University and assists with police investigations.

Though the tone of the poems consistently unsettles the reader, Walkington's imagination keeps her reader gripped. 'At Large', the opening poem, describes 'the bad people' who 'go through your cupboards' yet are 'mostly still at large, going about their business/ Shopping at the big Tesco [...]/ Waiting in line at the petrol station'. Her ability to be comical while creating an emotive impact is again exemplified in 'Happy families' which references the TV series: 'I see the Knezevics everywhere. They are the window cleaners casing/ the joint, or they're lurking in Audis'.

'Lies' are the focus of several poems. 'The last lie I told was in the eighties' ('Serial Liar'); 'Today is the last in a week of lies' ('Hatton Garden'); 'Lies the dog has told me' – dogs also appear in many poems, such as: 'There's a dog at the door [...] he wants our sausages, and he's got a warrant to take them' ('Utility Breed').

Walkington's voice is distinctive and assured, and her endings impactful. 'Utility Breed', in which 'the dog has taken to offering unsolicited advice', ends: 'The dog reassures me. / I will be able to tell/ when a man has rolled in something.' In her poems animal and human often share traits, but the closing poem, 'Ducks', develops this trope such that the speaker who is caring for some ducks is transformed. 'The neighbours become inquisitive' as her kitchen becomes a pond, wonderfully ending this enjoyable pamphlet:

> We roost on the granite island
> caked with poo. Our breath one rhythm, our feathers puffed.
> The two drakes lie awake longer than the rest,
> perched on the knife block, blinking into the night.

Glyn Maxwell
The Big Calls
Live Canon, £10

The year he was judging the T.S. Eliot prize Glyn Maxwell commented 'there aren't enough political poems'. Perhaps to redress this or provide an example, he has penned this formidable book.

There's always been a close relationship between politics and poetry, with poetic devices deployed in political speeches, not always for good, though as Nick Laird says: 'You can't write a political poem if it's just about politics.' The secret, as Seamus Heaney, who avoided being on either side in the Troubles, showed, is to write from the human experience. Maxwell does far more than this: his poems shadow some of the most famous of the English literary canon. This serves not just to echo a past that has created our current society and remind us that history repeats itself, but 'to praise, to lament, to inform, to enchant, to attack, to remind, to warn'[1].

Each poem carries a note identifying the classical poem that inspired it and detailing how the form is followed. Thus the poems can be enjoyed at many levels. For example, 'Burden' is after Kipling's 'The White Man's Burden', originally written for Queen Victoria's Diamond Jubilee, then revised and sent to Theodore Roosevelt as an exhortation to the US Government to colonise what were then the Philippine islands. Maxwell's poem shadows 'the rhyme, metre and length' of the Kipling original poem to chart the UK's flight from Kabul, in August 2021, and his poem ends impactfully:

> Boys, you did your damnedest
> the way you always do,
> and it's almost always murder
> and almost always you.

There are poems about Grenfell Tower, the coronavirus pandemic, police actions, murder, mental health issues and other issues.

---

[1] Foreword, p. 5, Glyn Maxwell, *The Big Calls,* Live Canon, 2023

Maxwell explains his choices came as visual images. My favourite is the opening poem in which, Maxwell recounts the cover-up in Kenya of a murder by a British soldier of a woman who was found lying in water. For Maxwell this evoked Tennyson's 'Lady of Shalott'. The poem chillingly ends:

> and nothing change. Diplomacy
> makes nothing happen, just like me,
> like thoughts and prayers and poetry
> and anything we do for free
>   in dwindling Camelot,
> this infinitely shrinking isle
> where you can zoom a google mile
> to find the wines-and-spirits aisle
>   where walks Sir Lancelot.

This is a big book, both playful and serious, that deserves to be read by anyone who cares.

Luke Samuel Yates
Dynamo
smith|doorstop, £6

The title of this debut collection which was a winner of the PBS 2022 prize suggests movement, yet 'The world is such a big hamster ball' ('Short-term lets') and Yates occupies himself with where this movement leads. This is 'A planet of traffic jams. Going somewhere/ but also not going anywhere', he writes in 'Going somewhere'. In 'Snorkelling', 'The sea was half on half off the beach'. He finds many ways to consider this paradox. 'She's never liked insects but that isn't the same as wanting/ 81% to have been eliminated globally in the last 30 years.' ('Flight mode').

His deadpan humour and fragmentary, quick-fire writing in response to everyday events at times recalls Frank O'Hara: 'the only thing to do is simply continue/ is that simple/ yes, it is simple because it is the only thing to do'.[2]

I particularly enjoyed 'Birmingham New Street has ten different exits' with its run-on: 'and all of them go to Birmingham'. In this poem,

---

[2] https://www.poetryfoundation.org/poems/57555/adieu-to-norman-bon-jour-to-joan-and-jean-paul

'I give a quid to a man who asks'; later he writes 'The guy I gave a pound to has probably/ already turned his life around.'

The speaker sees a seagull 'gliding around in thermal air currents of modest hope and disappointment.// 'Birmingham,'/ it calls. 'Birmingham,/ Birmingham, Birmingham'. A brilliant ending which has an echo of Vanessa Lampert's 'Canada'.

Sometimes the surreal takes off, such as in 'The pair of scissors that could cut anything': 'We saw them suddenly in the kitchen one day/ standing up'. And his images are good: 'horses grazing on their shadows' ('Going somewhere'); 'the Spanish plane trees/ lined up so close/ they had grown tall and graceful as librarians' ('Somehow I had written the times down wrong').

The collection is in three parts and interwoven in this is a relationship. In the title poem, ending the first section: 'I said yes, that I loved her, she said she loved me,/ I said goodbye, she said goodbye, that she loved me, I loved her,/ I said goodbye, bye bye bye byebyebye.' By the third section ('They're quite famous actually,') this relationship seems to have ended:

> Suddenly she's moving out
> and I'm getting into swimming.
> Up and down the pool I go, plunging my head
> again and again into the water

I love the humour of this book, and the closing words of the last poem seem to sum up the poet's take on life, 'Laundry': 'Drying, folding, putting away.'

Jane Clarke
A Change in the Air
Bloodaxe, £10.99

This collection is rooted in the natural world of Ireland where the poet grew up. Divided into six sections, it explores memory and loss. Bookended by the narrator's remembered childhood on a Roscommon farm and subsequent life in Wicklow, the intermediary sections recall Ireland's past, such as the troubles, emigration, mining in Wicklow and the first world war. This last section, taken from Clarke's pamphlet[3], felt

---

[3] Jane Clarke, *All the Way Home*, smith/doorstop, 2019

slightly less satisfying, being situated in France, and at times it was unclear who the speaker was, although soldiers dig graves, 'wielding pickaxe, mattock, spade// thinking of his grandad - / digging potatoes' ('Bouchavesnes'). However, the subsequent section firmly relocates the reader, following the course of the River Foyle.

This river poem is particularly interesting, not least by being in ten sextets, in contrast to the couplets employed in most of the collection; it also lies at the heart of the book. Perhaps to fully appreciate 'You could say it all begins' requires some knowledge of the terrain, but the place names themselves are musical: 'trails the Black River/ to the head of Lough Macneen Upper,/ crosses the lake to the Belcoo River mouth'. Following this is the only poem written in free form. 'Crossings' is a list poem of images floating across ten lines, creating a 360 degree view: 'a coffin path   a stile in a drystone wall   a pass between two peaks'.

Clarke's precision and clean lines, together with her detailing of domestic life set against historical events, brought to mind Eavan Boland: in 'Flight', set in the Troubles, neighbours helped the family load 'mattresses, blankets, rugs, cups and saucers,/ wrapped in tea towels, a can of milk/ gifts of cabbage and soda bread.' as they left, 'family bible at their feet.'

I particularly enjoyed the pared-back titles, juxtaposed with Clarke's fine lyricism, such as in 'Eggs': 'she poured fresh water/ and ladled corn into the dented tin dish,/ adding handfuls of seeds and grit'; and in 'Mullacor', 'To drink from the stream that rings silver/ through gorse and fraughan to the Mill Brook waterwheel'.

The collection exudes the poet's love for the natural world, for her wife to whom the book is dedicated: 'I practise saying *Isobel is my wife*/ and it sings to the tune of my life' ('Wife'), and for Wicklow where the couple settle: 'The house looked like home that evening in May; honeysuckle tangled in hazel'.

Kris Johnson
Ghost River
Bloodaxe, £10.99

This debut collection is steeped in deep ecology and a fascination for the land that exists beneath naming and mapping. Johnson grew up in Washington, US, in lands charted by George Vancouver during his expedition to locate a Northwest Passage. In the title poem the poet writes

> beneath the homestead
> of my ancestors [...]
>
> beneath the K-Mart
> and the Walmart,
> Valley Highway [...]
>
> there are ghost rivers
> from which we all drink

The central section of the book focusses on the legacy of Vancouver, his naming of Mount Rainier, Baker and other places after friends and colleagues. In 'George Vancouver, you are not my father' the poet writes 'though where would I be without you?/ Everywhere I once was, you are, forever.'

The speaker wonders how the landscape first appeared to Vancouver: 'he's thinking about trees,/ their impossible tallness, their beautiful utility/ What keels they could be, what masts' ('Church'). Then in 'Small Distances' imagining him differently:

> I see you with a scattering
> of children harvesting
> geoducks and salmon berries
> on the shadow of the firs.

This central section, titled 'Passage', also carries an echo of childbirth, for concurrent with Johnson's anthropocene writings, are themes of motherhood, humanity's place on earth and grief.

These are peopled landscapes. In 'Skinny Dip' the narrator imagines swimming in a lake where 'those beautiful boys/ drowned earlier in the summer', and feeling 'their tongues, strong from great mouthfuls of water, licking my neck,'. Her immediate family is also present. The collection opens: 'I am in love with this mountain/ that all summer long threatens to kill// my father.' ('Rainier') – her father seemingly enjoyed mountaineering. The final poem has the stunning image of the narrator holding water 'the way you might hold your daughter's hair./ Braiding water is easier if you close your eyes.'

Finally, these are poems about movement and stillness. 'I used to believe the purpose/ of life was movement' Johnson writes, 'I never stopped to consider/ the mountain's stillness/ only its power' ('Tectronics'). The book ends with an image of the poet's grandmother swimming in a pool, 'her body forever in motion.' These are musical, lyrical poems that evoke the majesty of landscape, the depth and power of water and invite us to stop, and look again.

Hilary Llewellyn-Williams
The Little Hours: New and Selected Poems
Seren, £12.99

Llewellyn-Williams's latest collection includes poems from *The Tree Calendar, Book of Shadows, Animaculture* and *Greenland* as well as the new poems of *The Little Hours*, which follow a gap in publication of twenty years during which time the poet developed a psychotherapy practice.

Llewellyn-Williams's style remains highly recognisable, employing the same lyricism, rich observations and strong narratorial voice. In an early poem, 'Death Day', the speaker's grandmother is 'like a virgin laid in her snow;/ her face fine with a feathery softness'. The poet's recent 'Hens in the Yard' tells of 'Your childhood rested deep/ in its stones, a spider tracery,/ papery and frail, little breaths of dust'.

Death, together with an interest in the spirit world, is a recurrent theme. If there is a tonal shift, possibly the more recent poems seem more melancholic. In the second section of 'A Long Goodbye', dedicated to her husband who died in 2018, Llewellyn-Williams writes there is 'nothing to keep the dark/ from seeping in' and the poem touchingly ends: 'My love surrounds you as long as I stay breathing.'

Most of Llewellyn-Williams's collections include a sequence. In 'Book of Shadows' she synthesises Giordano Bruni's writings with images from Tarot, while the gorgeous 'Tree Calendar' is inspired by Robert Graves's *The White Goddess*. The sequence in 'The Little Hours' refers to the shorter Canonical Hours from the Rule of St Benedict and read like little meditations. In '*Prime*', the poet looks out the window, 'where fine gauze waters, pearly weft/ stretched taut and still' ('Sea View') as she muses upon

> The world piled up at my back
> like memory
>
> and before me just this blank
> sky, the thin worn-out hedge
> tossed on the breeze and the barrier of sea.
>
> Well I can't go back, I'm here now

This use of 'Well' is a Llewellyn-Williams trope that recurs throughout the book, inviting the reader to feel directly addressed. Occasionally her writing veers towards the whimsical, such as 'Out With My Broomstick' ('the stick itself is long and extends behind me/ ready for the children to clamber on') but this is balanced by an earthy humour in others: 'Well if I know God She's no/ housewife. She'd rather dance/ than sit with a lap of apples' ('A Lap of Apples').

Love, grief, nature and liminal spaces are subject matters, together with seeing the spiritual within the natural: 'The imminent and omnipresent hills/ which were always there, during Lauds and Vespers,/ a mighty unseen eminence, like God' ('Llanthony Priory'). These are lovely thought-provoking reflections on life, loss, and love.

Mary Mulholland

Contributors

Sharon Ashton is a poet and novelist who lives in Shropshire. She was one of four runners-up in this year's *Telegraph* Poetry Competition, and her poems have appeared in *The Interpreter's House* and *The Rialto*. More of her writing can be found at: sharonashtonpoetry.com

Julian Bishop's first collection of eco-poems, called, *We Saw It All Happen* is published by Fly on the Wall Press (2023). Formerly environment reporter for the BBC, he has been a runner-up in the Gingko Prize for Eco Poetry.

Claire Booker lives near Brighton. Her poems have recently appeared in *Agenda, Dreamcatcher, Fenland Poetry Journal* and *Magma*. One of her poems, set to music, will be performed as part of 'Between The Lines' at this year's Edinburgh Festival. Her collection *A Pocketful of Chalk* is out with Arachne Press.

Caspar Bryant is a poet from West Cornwall. Their work can be found in *SPAM zine, Broken Sleep, Ink Sweat & Tears, Deleuzine* and *Propel Magazine*. He currently lives in Fife.

Matt Bryden is a poet and teacher living in Devon. He has published a pamphlet *Night Porter* (Templar, 2010), a first collection *Boxing the Compass* (Templar, 2013) and more recently a pamphlet *The Glassblower's House* (Live Canon, 2023).

Matthew Caley has published six collections. His seventh, *To Abandon Wizardry*, is published by Bloodaxe in November 2023. He's currently Associate Lecturer in Creative Writing at the University of St Andrews.

Jane Campbell a multi-award-winning dyke poet has recently won the 2022 Disability Arts Cymru creative writing award for her poem 'Aroused'. She is a new-phase poet, having her first collection published aged 57. Winner of the 2021 Geoff Stevens Memorial Poetry Prize with her debut collection *Slowly as Clouds*.

Diana Cant is a poet and child psychotherapist. Her poems have been published in various anthologies and magazines, including *Agenda, The North* and *Poetry News*. Her most recent pamphlet, *At Risk – the lives some children live*, was published by Dempsey and Windle in 2021. She has been nominated for the Forward Prize for best individual poem, 2023, and is the winner of the Plaza Prize.

Deb Catesby has been writing poems for the past two years, taking a series of courses with the Poetry School and with Arvon. She is also a painter, working from her studio on the Hereford/Worcester borders. Previously she wrote plays and taught Creative Writing to degree level to mature students.

Marc Chamberlain is a poet and critic. His work has appeared in titles including *The Times Literary Supplement, The Mechanics' Institute Review, Magma, The Hudson Review* and *The Best New British and Irish Poets 2019-2021*. He is based in London and is a Creative Writing PhD Candidate at Durham University.

Alexandra Corrin-Tachibana's first collection, *Sing me down from the dark,* was published by SALT in 2022 and is already in its second issue. Her poems are widely published including in *PN Review, The North, Poetry Wales, The Moth* and *Fenland Poetry Journal.*

Lesley Curwen is a poet and sailor living in Plymouth. She was highly commended in the Poetry Wales Award and has had a collaborative pamphlet published by Nine Pens Press.

Ann Cuthbert is 70. She began writing when she retired. Her work has been published in many magazines and anthologies. She performs with Tees Women Poets and runs a monthly spoken word night for older writers. Her chapbook, *Watching a Heron with Davey,* is published by BLER Press.

Hélène Demetriades' debut collection *The Plumb Line*, was published by Hedgehog Press in 2022. She is a psychotherapist and lives in South Devon. Published in magazines and anthologies, and placed in competitions, she won The Silver Wyvern, Poetry On The Lake, 2022.

Steve Denehan lives in Kildare, Ireland with his wife Eimear and daughter Robin. He is the author of two chapbooks and four poetry collections. Winner of the Anthony Cronin Poetry Award and twice winner of Irish Times' *New Irish Writing*, his numerous publication credits include *Poetry Ireland Review* and *Westerly*.

Neil Douglas worked as a GP and Community Paediatrician and is currently a student of Life and Creative Writing at Goldsmiths, University of London. He has published in magazines and anthologies in the UK, North America and Hong Kong.

Sarah Doyle is the Pre-Raphaelite Society's Poet-in-Residence. She has been published widely and placed in many competitions. Her pamphlet *Something so wild and new in this feeling* was published by V. Press in 2021, while *(m)othersongs* is forthcoming in autumn 2023 from the same publisher. More at: sarahdoyle.co.uk

Philip Dunkerley is active in poetry groups in the South Lincolnshire area, where he lives. He likes to inflict his poems on others at open mic events, and his stuff has slipped past the editors of quite a few journals, anthologies and webzines – including those of *The Alchemy Spoon*.

Elaine Ewart is a poet and writer of creative non-fiction based in North Yorkshire. Her poetry has been published in various anthologies and journals, including *The Interpreter's House, Arc Poetry Magazine* and *Ink, Sweat & Tears*. Her travel memoir, *Heligoland*, is forthcoming with Muscaliet Press in autumn 2023.

Pascal Fallas is a writer and (occasional) photographer currently living in Norfolk, UK. His poems have recently appeared in *The North, Lighthouse, London Grip* and *Cerasus* among other places. For more information/contact please visit www.pascalfallas.com.

Martin Ferguson's first pamphlet was shortlisted by Against the Grain Press and published in 2019 by Original Plus. He has been widely published in UK poetry magazines. He lives and works in France and was guest poet on Paris Spoken World Online, hosted by Canadian musician and poet, David Sirois.

Jen Feroze lives by the sea in Essex. A former Foyle Young Poet, her work has recently appeared in publications including *Stanchion, Poetry Wales, OneArt* and *Spelt*. She was a winner of the 2022/2023 *Magma* Editors' Prize, and her debut pamphlet is forthcoming with Nine Pens.

Viv Fogel's poems have appeared in magazines and anthologies since the mid-70's. Her second collection, *Imperfect Beginnings* (2023), is published by award-winning Fly on the Wall Press. London-based, Viv lives with her partner, is a psychotherapist, mentor, artist, ex-teacher and community worker, and a grandmother who still loves to dance.

Victoria Gatehouse is a zoologist based in the Pennines. She came to poetry in mid-life, after a career in science. Her poems have been widely published in magazines and anthologies and placed in many competitions. Victoria's pamphlet *The Mechanics of Love*, published by smith|doorstop, was selected as a Laureate's Choice.

SK Grout (she/they) is an editor and writer who grew up in Aotearoa New Zealand, lived in Germany, and now splits her time between London and Auckland Tamaki Makaurau. Her debut chapbook: *What love would smell like* (V.Press, 2021). https://skgroutpoetry.wixsite.com/poetry

Jake Wild Hall founded publisher Bad Betty in 2017. He is the author of pamphlets, *Blank* (2019) and *Solomon's World* (2016, Saboteur Awards Best Pamphlet longlist). He has been published in journals, online magazines and anthologies including *bath magg* and Broken Sleep's *Hit Points*.

Chris Hardy has travelled widely. After years in London, he lives in Sussex. His poems have been published in magazines, anthologies, online, and have been highly commended and shortlisted in the Poetry Society, Live Canon and other competitions. Chris's new collection *KEY TO THE HIGHWAY* is published by Shoestring Press.

Tamsin Hopkins writes poetry and fiction. She has an MA in Creative Writing from Royal Holloway and is a previous winner of The Aesthetica Prize. Poems have appeared in *Mslexia, The London Magazine, Magma*, and *The Alchemy Spoon*. Her pamphlet *Inside the Smile* is published by Cinnamon Press.

Wendy Klein has three published collections: *Cuba in The Blood* and *Anything in Turquoise*, (Cinnamon Press, 2009 and 2013), *Mood Indigo*, (Oversteps Books, 2016); and a Selected: *Out of the Blue* (The High Window Press, 2019).

Wendy Kyle is poet and reviewer, published in *Mslexia, Poetry Salzburg, Interpreters House*; *Poetry International Quarterly, The Tangerine*. Most recently, in *Blackbox Manifold, Anthropocene* and *Alternative Field Anthology* (2022). She has been shortlisted in many international prizes including the National Poetry Competition (2018) and was runner up in Mslexia Women's Poetry Prize (2019).

Robin Houghton's work appears widely in magazines. She was awarded the Hamish Canham Prize in 2013 and has won or been placed in numerous competitions. Her fourth pamphlet, WHY? AND OTHER QUESTIONS, was a joint winner of the 2019 Live Canon Poetry Pamphlet Competition. robinhoughtonpoetry.co.uk | planetpoetrypodcast.com

Sue Lewis began reading and writing poetry as a way of finding her voice and confidence after a mid-life stroke. She has twice won the Cinnamon Press Pamphlet Award: in 2019 with *Texture* and again in 2021 with *Journey*. In 2022 she was shortlisted for the Bridport Poetry prize.

Caroline Maldonado has five poetry collections translated from Italian (Smokestack Books, 2013-22). Her own poetry has appeared in magazines, including, *Agenda, Tears in the Fence, Shearsman*, online and in anthologies. Her publications are *What they say in Avenale* (IDP 2014) and *Faultlines* (Vole Books, 2022).

Jennifer A. McGowan is a Forward and Pushcart-prize nominated poet and prefers the 15th century to the 21st, though she comes back for indoor plumbing.

Cos Michael wrote poetry when younger, but paused, distracted by the need to earn a living. Recently, having sorted out her priorities, she started writing again. Her themes explore growing up and life now, from an autistic perspective. She has had poems published by *Grindstone* and *Atrium.*

Elizabeth Chadwick Pywell's latest pamphlet, *Breaking (Out)*, was published by Selcouth Station. She has been published in journals including *Fourteen Poems* and *New Welsh Review*, longlisted for the Mslexia Women's Poetry Competition, shortlisted for the Ironbridge Festival Prize and won the Northern Writers' Debut Award for Poetry: Out-Spoken Press Programme.

Gillie Robic was born in India. Puppeteer and voice in film, theatre and television, her poems appear in many magazines and anthologies. Her poetry collections, *Swimming Through Marble* and *Lightfalls,* are published by Live Canon, also her pamphlet *Open Skies*, in aid of Ukraine. A third collection is due this year.

Sula Rubens R.W.S. studied at Central/St. Martin's School of Art (BA Hons Fine Art). She has collaborated with artists, poets and musicians nationally and internationally. In 2019 she was elected by the Royal Watercolour Society to become an Associate Member. In 2022 she was honoured with full membership.

Finola Scott's work finds shelter in various nests including *New Writing Scotland, Spelt, Lighthouse* and *Gutter*. Politics, environment and relationships concern her. Although she knows poetry won't change the world, she writes compulsively. A slam-winning Granny, she has three publications. She welcomes you to FB Finola Scott Poems.

Jean Sprackland is a poet and writer. She is the winner of the Costa Poetry Award in 2008, and the Portico Prize for Non-Fiction in 2012. Her books have also been shortlisted for the Forward Prize, the T.S. Eliot Prize and the PEN Ackerley Prize. Jean is Professor of Creative Writing at Manchester Metropolitan University and a Fellow of the Royal Society of Literature.

Martha Sprackland is an editor, writer and translator. Founder-editor of independent publisher Offord Road Books, and previously an editor for Faber and for *Poetry London*, she now runs the poetry list for CHEERIO Publishing. Martha is a trustee for the Rebecca Swift Foundation and an Arvon tutor. Her collection *Citadel* (Pavilion Poetry, 2020) was shortlisted for both the Forward Prize for Best First Collection and the Costa Poetry Award.

Laura Stanley is a poet from the West Midlands. Her heresy has been published in *bath magg, Magma, The Interpreter's House, After Sylvia* (Nine Arches Press) and by the Young Poets Network.

Julie Stevens writes poems that cover many themes, but often engages with the problems of disability. She has two published pamphlets: *Balancing Act* (The Hedgehog Poetry Press, 2021) and *Quicksand* (Dreich, 2020). Her next collection will be *Step into the Dark* (The Hedgehog Poetry Press).

Jeffery Sugarman is an American-born poet in London. He was a 2019 Jerwood/Arvon mentee with Hannah Lowe and is published in *Present Tense, Magma* and *Finished Creatures*; his debut chapbook, *Dear Friend(s),* explores kinship and loss, particularly during the early AIDS epidemic of the 1990s, available from The Emma Press.

Anne Symons began writing poetry in retirement. Her work has appeared in a range of publications in print and online. She was recently awarded second prize in the Gloucestershire Open Poetry Competition. Anne has completed an MA in Writing Poetry at Newcastle University and the Poetry School in London.

Lesley Sharpe teaches literature and creative writing in London. Her poems and essays have been published in *Aesthetica, The Alchemy Spoon, Dragons of the Prime* (Emma Press) and *Finished Creatures*, shortlisted for the London Magazine, Aesthetica and Bridport prizes. She edits *Heron* magazine for the Katherine Mansfield Society and is a co-founder of Lodestone Poets.

Dave Wakely has worked as a musician, university administrator, poetry librarian and editor. His writing has appeared in several magazines and anthologies. He lives in Buckinghamshire with his husband and too many books, CDs and guitars. He tweets as @theverbalist.

Sue Wallace-Shaddad has an MA in Poetry from Newcastle University. Her latest book, *Sleeping Under Clouds,* a collaboration with artist Sula Rubens, was published by Clayhanger Press, April 2023. Dempsey & Windle published her pamphlet *A City Waking Up* (2020). Sue is Secretary of Suffolk Poetry Society. suewallaceshaddad.wordpress.com

Zoë Wells is a poet from Suffolk, based in London. She is a postgraduate student of Creative Writing at the University of Cambridge and is a member of the East Suffolk Poets Workshop Group. She is currently working on her first pamphlet *Clay Bodies* and the narrative epic *At Sea*.

Judith Wozniak has an MA in Writing Poetry. Her poems have appeared in, *The Alchemy Spoon, Fenland Poetry Journal, The Frogmore Papers, London Grip* and *Ink Sweat & Tears.* She won first prize in the Hippocrates Competition 2020. Her pamphlet, *Patient Watching*, was published by The Hedgehog Press in 2022.

The Alchemy Spoon pamphlet competition 2023

The competition will be judged by Chris Hardy

The winner will receive a publishing contract with Clayhanger Press and 25 free printed copies of the pamphlet and an online Zoom book launch. The prize pamphlet will contain 24 to 32 pages of poetry.

Opens 1 August 2023. Closing date: 31 October 2023

Entries for the competition should be as a single file containing between 8 and 10 poems that showcase the poet's work.

- All poems must be entirely the entrant's own work. Individual poems in an entry may have been published online, in journals or magazines, or multi-author anthologies, provided the writer retains copyright.
- Each entry should contain 8 to 10 poems of no more than 70 lines per poem including stanza breaks. Each poem should start on a new page and be in 12 pt Times Roman font.
- Winners will be invited to submit up to 32 pages of poetry for their pamphlet.
- You may submit up to two entries, each of 8–10 poems, provided an entry fee is paid for each.
- Your entry's title should appear on a separate first page. The title may relate to a key poem or suggest the collection's theme if it has one. The title must also be the name of the file containing your poems.
- To maintain anonymous judging, there must be no identifying marks on any poem or title page. We will match your entry title to your email address after anonymous judging is complete.
- Each entry must have all the poems in one file in Word format. If possible, please set the page size to A5 format or 6 x 8 inches.
- Simultaneous submissions are accepted, but an entry must be withdrawn in the event of it winning a prize or publication elsewhere.
- Results will be emailed by January 31 2024 to all who entered, and published on the *Alchemy Spoon* website shortly afterwards.
- The entry fee will be £10 each.
- Entries must be paid for, and your entry file uploaded, by the closing time of 11.59 pm on 31 October 2023.

Full details of the competition and the link to enter your submission can be found on *The Alchemy Spoon* website and on Duotrope

Submission Guidelines

We welcome submissions of up to three brilliant, unpublished, original poems on the issue's theme through the website during the submission window. You will find full details of how to submit on our website: www.alchemyspoon.org.

We are only able to accept submissions from those over 18.

If you have poems published in the current issue of *The Alchemy Spoon*, then we ask that you wait out one issue before submitting more work.

Simultaneous submissions are permitted but please tell us straightaway if a poem is accepted for publication elsewhere.

We aim for a speedy turnaround and will respond to every submission, but we don't offer individual feedback.

Authors retain all rights. However, if a poem is then published elsewhere, please acknowledge that it first appeared in *The Alchemy Spoon*.

Our submission window for Issue 11 will be open 1 – 30 September 2023, the theme for the issue will be 'Colours' and we will welcome poems on this theme up to 40 lines. See our website for the full details.

Submission Guidelines for Essays
If you have an essay on some cutting-edge poetry-related topic, please send it to us during the submission window for consideration +/- 1500 words.

Submission Guidelines for Artwork
We are always looking for original artwork to feature on future magazine covers. Portrait-orientated images work best (or images suitable for cropping). Good quality lower resolution images can be sent at the submission stage, but higher res files will be needed (2480 pixels x 3508 pixels) at print stage. Please email us with your images as an attachment.

Submission Guidelines for Reviews
If you would like to recommend a poetry collection or submit a review of a collection, then please email us or use the contact form on the website.

Poetry Workshops
The Alchemy Spoon editors offer a one-to-one poetry feedback and workshopping service without prejudice via Zoom or Facetime. All profits from this contribute to the cost of running Clayhanger Press. Please email requests for feedback to: vanessa.tas@btinternet.com to arrange this.

Cover Design by Clayhanger Press

Typesetting and Design Roger Bloor
Senior Copy Editor Sara Levy
Proof-reader Adam Lampert

www.clayhangerpress.co.uk

www.ingramcontent.com/pod-product-compliance
Lightning Source LLC
Chambersburg PA
CBHW042117100526
44587CB00025B/4095